The Remarkable Journey of the
MORMON BATTALION

Front cover images: top, *Mormon Battalion* by George M. Ottinger. Bottom images from left to right, *Tucson*, Courtesy of the Charles L. Camp Collection of Stereographs, Bancroft Library. *Battalion Veterans*, Courtesy of Church History Library. *B. Y. Calling Volunteers for the Mormon Battalion* by C. C. A. Christensen. *Thomas L. Kane*, Courtesy of the Library of Congress. *Santa Fe* by Curtis B. Graham, courtesy of Beinecke Rare Book and Manuscript Library, Yale University. Back cover image, *Mormon Battalion Ball, July 1846* by C. C. A. Christensen. Chapter heads images: Detail of *Mapa de los Estados Unidos de Mejico* courtesy of the Library of Congress. Front endsheet image: *Mapa de los Estados Unidos de Mejico* courtesy of the Library of Congress.

Cover and book design copyright © 2012 by Covenant Communications, Inc.

Published by Covenant Communications, Inc.
American Fork, Utah

Printed in China
First Printing: September 2012

18 17 16 15 14 13 12   10 9 8 7 6 5 4 3 2 1

ISBN 978-1-62108-130-2

History of the Saints

The Remarkable Journey of the

MORMON BATTALION

Michael N. Landon & Brandon J. Metcalf

ACKNOWLEDGMENTS

We as authors gratefully acknowledge a number of individuals without whose help this volume would not have been possible. In particular, we thank Glenn Rawson and Dennis Lyman, producers of the series, History of the Saints, for suggesting the project and encouraging us to write this history of the Mormon Battalion. Our colleagues at the Church History Library, William W. Slaughter and April Williamsen, assisted us in countless ways during our effort to finish the book; we will always be grateful for their help. We also wish to thank Kathryn Jenkins Gordon, Margaret Weber, Mark Sorenson, and the entire staff at Covenant Communications for their constant encouragement and remarkable talents in helping us bring the book to life. Finally, we appreciate the staff of the Church History Library and the archival and library professionals of many other repositories who gave their time and assistance to us. In particular, we thank Russ Taylor at Brigham Young University, and Walter Jones and Elizabeth Rogers at the University of Utah Marriott Library.

We give special thanks to our families, who often sacrificed their own interests in allowing us the opportunity to write about the remarkable journey of the Mormon Battalion. To Brandon's wife, Angela, caring for four children, and Mike's wife, Loretta, caring for her mother and her mother-in-law, we convey our deepest gratitude.

In writing this volume, we were enriched as we studied and reflected on this unusual American military unit. In very personal terms, we will always be grateful to those who served in or were associated with the Mormon Battalion.

We feel a strong commitment to insuring that the work be as accurate as possible, but as a friend of ours once remarked, "Doctors bury their mistakes; authors publish theirs." Any errors found herein are ours and we also acknowledge that we are solely responsible for the content of this volume.

Michael N. Landon
Brandon J. Metcalf
Salt Lake City, Utah
September 2012

FOREWORD

In December 1847, Reddick Allred and other men of the Mormon Battalion, having completed their voluntary service in the United States Army, made their way into the Latter-day Saint settlement of Kanesville, Iowa, seeking their families. Their service and return had been fraught with much difficulty, and there was much rejoicing and reunion on their return.

President Brigham Young proclaimed a jubilee celebration at the Log Tabernacle in their honor. Reddick and his companion, William Hyde, made their way to the celebration, as recorded in Reddick's diary: "As Brother William Hyde and I were approaching, President Young said to President Kimball and others (pointing to us), 'These men were the salvation of this Church.'"

The service of the Mormon Battalion was groundbreaking—indeed, seminal. Not only did Brigham Young consider the offering of the Battalion as a salvation to the Latter-day Saints at a critical time in their history, but so too did the men of the Mormon Battalion shape so much of the history of the United States. Theirs is a fascinating story too long neglected and too little understood.

For that reason, History of the Saints is pleased to introduce this unique and timely volume chronicling the story of the Mormon Battalion. Through compelling narrative and rich visuals, the history of the Mormon Battalion comes to life with all of its faith, sacrifice, and unflagging service. The story of these men and women is at once humbling and inspiring.

Authors Michael Landon and Brandon Metcalf bring together a lifetime of scholarship, skill, and insight to present this work. You will be drawn in and sense that a work such as this cannot be brought forth with just the reading of a few books and the collecting of a few photos. This is a volume worthy of generations.

We hope this story touches you as much as it has us.

Glenn Rawson
Dennis Lyman
Bryant Bush
Salt Lake City, Utah
September 2012

TABLE OF CONTENTS

Painting by C. C. A. Christensen depicting the recruitment of the Mormon Battalion.

PREFACE

The march of nearly five hundred Mormon volunteers from Council Bluffs, Iowa Territory, to the Pacific coast of Alta California from 1846–1847 is well known in the annals of Mormon history. While lesser known to the general public, their march of nearly two thousand miles by foot is an important component in understanding the Mexican War and the westward expansion of the United States. Members of the Mormon Battalion endured hardship and sacrificed much in the name of their religion. Unique in American military history, the Mormon Battalion represents the only American military unit mustered into service based solely on religious affiliation. The call for a battalion came at a turbulent time in Mormon history when leaders of The Church of Jesus Christ of Latter-day Saints were focused on fleeing the United States, not joining her in a border dispute with Mexico.

With numerous books and articles published about the Mormon Battalion, it may seem that the story has been told and needs no further examination. We have written this book with a few objectives in mind that separate it from previous works. Intended for general readership, this volume provides a foot-on-the-ground experience with a primary focus on the 333 men and four women that completed the march to the coast.[1] (The approximately 150 men who were detached from service and wintered at Pueblo, as well as the women and children who traveled with them, are not highlighted in these pages. Their remarkable experience deserves a treatment of its own that is beyond the scope of the current volume.) What was it like to be a member of the Mormon Battalion? What did they experience day to day? What effect did the march have on the men? These are questions we wanted more complete answers to from the outset. In seeking to understand the individual soldier's experience, we have relied heavily on the voices of the Battalion, consulting both contemporaneous writings as well as retrospective accounts in hopes that the story might resonate more fully within the mind of the reader.

The Battalion never participated in any combat with Mexican forces during the war. Despite oft-repeated claims, they did not complete the longest overland march in history. As an example, Alexander the Great led a march of more than twenty thousand miles in a single decade.[2] The real contribution of the Mormon Battalion came through opening the first wagon road to the Pacific, helping establish U.S. military control of what is today southern California, and through assisting their fellow Latter-day Saints migrate to the Salt Lake Valley with the funds they received. After their discharge from the U.S. Army, the former Mormon soldiers continued to make history by participating in the gold discovery at Coloma that started California's historic Gold Rush, blazing the Carson route over the Sierra Nevada Mountains, establishing Hensley's Salt Lake Cutoff as a viable wagon route, and guiding the first wagons over the Spanish Trail. Moreover, the yearlong military experience brought the men maturity, developed skills and talents, and created a self-confidence in many of these men that enabled them to later lead and serve as colonizers, captain pioneer companies bound for Utah Territory, serve as missionaries, and become legislative and civic leaders in states and communities throughout the West. Clearly, this would not have occurred without their volunteer enlistment and subsequent military service in the Mormon Battalion.

What began as a military march became a defining event in the lives of the hundreds of men who heeded the counsel of their Church leaders and enlisted in the hot summer of July 1846, leaving behind the comfort and familiarity of family and friends. Brigham Young credited the Battalion as the "temporal salvation of the Camp of Israel." It would be a year before the men were discharged from the army, just days prior to the first Mormon pioneer company reaching the Salt Lake Valley. During that year and during that seemingly endless march, some of the Battalion died, and scores of the sick and those deemed unfit to continue to the Pacific were detached to spend the winter in Fort Pueblo. The majority of those who completed the trek to the Pacific were young men. They returned to civilian life with a world view greatly expanded by countless experiences in places they had never been and with cultures and people dramatically different than any they had ever known before. In a fitting tribute, the third commander of the Mormon Battalion—Philip St. George Cooke—lauded the men in these words:

> History may be searched in vain for an equal
> march of infantry. Half of it has been through a wil-
> derness where nothing but savages and wild beasts
> are found, or deserts where, for want of water, there
> is no living creature. There, with almost hopeless

labor we have dug deep wells, which the future traveler will enjoy. Without a guide who had traversed them, we have ventured into trackless table-lands where water was not found for several marches. With crowbar and pick and axe in hand, we have worked our way over mountains, which seemed to defy aught save the wild goat, and hewed a passage through a chasm of living rock more narrow than our wagons. To bring these first wagons to the Pacific, we have preserved the strength of our mules by herding them over large tracts, which you have laboriously guarded without loss. The garrison of four presidios of Sonora concentrated within the walls of Tucson, gave us no pause. We drove them out, with their artillery, but our intercourse with the citizens was unmarked by a single act of injustice. Thus, marching half naked and half fed, and living upon wild animals, we have discovered and made a road of great value to our country.[3]

The authors are indebted to many historians whose significant contributions have brought a greater understanding of the story of the Mormon Battalion. John F. Yurtinus's 1975 dissertation, "A Ram in the Thicket: The Mormon Battalion in the Mexican War," remains essential as an exhaustive scholarly history on the subject. Norma Ricketts's volume, *The Mormon Battalion: U.S. Army of the West, 1846–1848*, published in 1996, is important for its day-by-day history of the march as well as the compilation and analysis of company rosters. In 2000, editors David L. Bigler and Will Bagley published numerous first-person accounts of Battalion members in *Army of Israel: Mormon Battalion Narratives*, an extremely useful work containing important and previously unpublished journals, reports, correspondence, and reminiscences. Finally, Sherman L. Fleek's volume, *History May Be Searched in Vain: A Military History of the Mormon Battalion*, published in 2006, provides an excellent analysis of the Battalion from a military perspective; Fleek is also the first historian to provide a balanced account of the non-Mormon surgeon assigned to the Battalion through his analysis of the journal of Dr. George B. Sanderson. These excellent works are indispensable in understanding the genesis, enlistment, march, contributions, and legacy of the Mormon Battalion.

While more than 160 years have passed since the epic march of the Battalion, the event still resonates today. For those living in the twenty-first century, surrounded by so many modern conveniences and accustomed to modes of transportation that allow travel over thousands of miles in a matter of hours, it is difficult to fully comprehend the mid-nineteenth-century experiences of the soldiers in the Mormon Battalion. Conceptually, journeying overland on foot across mostly unknown territory seems totally foreign to the present-day observer. The story of the Mormon Battalion—a story of faith, commitment, and sacrifice—transcends the passage of time. For generations, these universal principles, exhibited in the words and deeds of those in the Mormon Battalion, have helped strengthen the resolve of many in overcoming life's adversity. We hope that their story, briefly conveyed in the pages of this volume, will inspire others to reflect on the resilience of the human spirit; instill a deeper appreciation of the past; and provide courage, comfort, and hope to each of us as we face and strive to overcome our own long and arduous marches.

Endnotes

1   This number is found in Norma Baldwin Ricketts, *The Mormon Battalion: U.S. Army of the West, 1846–1848* (Logan: Utah State University Press, 1996), 278–282.

2   For information regarding military marches of greater distance than the Mormon Battalion see Sherman L. Fleek, *History May Be Searched in Vain: A Military History of the Mormon Battalion* (Spokane, WA: Arthur H. Clark Co., 2006), 324–327.

3   Philip St. George Cooke, "Orders No. 1," in Daniel S. Tyler, *A Concise History of the Mormon Battalion in the Mexican War, 1846–1847* (Salt Lake City, 1881), 254–255.

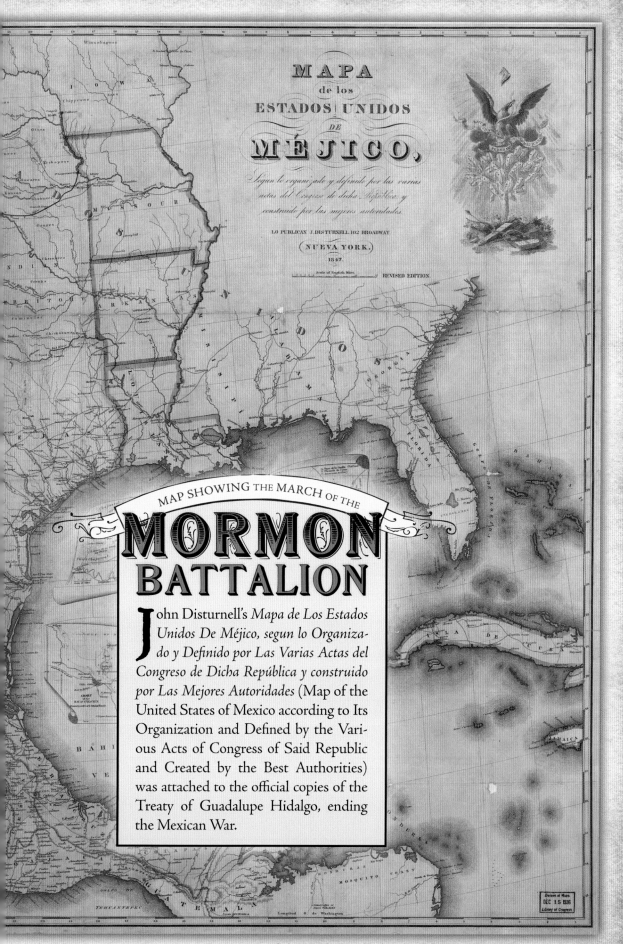

MAPA
de los
ESTADOS UNIDOS
DE
MÉJICO,

LO PUBLICAN J. DISTURNELL. 102 BROADWAY

(NUEVA YORK.)
1847.

REVISED EDITION.

MAP SHOWING THE MARCH OF THE

MORMON
BATTALION

John Disturnell's *Mapa de Los Estados Unidos De Méjico, segun lo Organizado y Definido por Las Varias Actas del Congreso de Dicha República y construido por Las Mejores Autoridades* (Map of the United States of Mexico according to Its Organization and Defined by the Various Acts of Congress of Said Republic and Created by the Best Authorities) was attached to the official copies of the Treaty of Guadalupe Hidalgo, ending the Mexican War.

Mapa de los Estados Unidos de Mejico courtesy of the Library of Congress.

Chapter One

TO THE MISSOURI RIVER

"A plot laid to bring trouble"

In mid-July 1846, members of The Church of Jesus Christ of Latter-day Saints were spread from east to west across 265 miles of Iowa beginning at Nauvoo, Illinois, along the Mississippi, all the way to Council Bluffs, bordering the Missouri River. Sustained persecution by local mobs forced the evacuation of Nauvoo, their "City Beautiful," earlier than anticipated.[1] This exodus from Nauvoo was another in a sequence of forced migrations experienced by Church members spanning a decade and a half, with some of the early converts moving from New York to northern Ohio and western Missouri before fleeing to Illinois in 1839. Leaving destitute from their homes and with minimal supplies, the first wave of Saints departed Nauvoo for the West beginning in early February 1846. Determined to distance themselves from the United States, they sought religious freedom and refuge from persecution. The Saints struggled across Iowa through what one diarist referred to as a "continuous mud hole" and established large camps along the Missouri River.[2] The group was malnourished, lacking supplies and clothing, and stricken with illness.

While in these difficult circumstances, representatives from the federal government entered the Mormon camps to enlist a five-hundred-member battalion to march toward Mexico and participate in the Mexican War that had commenced in April. Hosea Stout captured the apprehensive feelings shared by many of the Saints at the time, indignantly recording that the effort was "a plot laid to bring trouble" and that if "we did not comply with the requisition we supposed they would now make a protest to denounce us as enemies to our country and if we did not comply that they would then have 500 of our men in their power to be destroyed as they had done our leaders at Carthage. I confess that my feeling was uncommonly wrought up against them."[3] While many Church members were suspicious and angered by the request from the same government that had long neglected to intervene in their behalf over years of

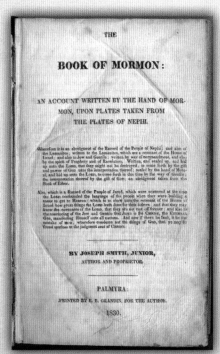

Joseph Smith Jr. (1805–1844), first prophet and president of The Church of Jesus Christ of Latter-day Saints. (Courtesy of Church History Library.)

Title page of the first edition of the Book of Mormon published in 1830 by E. B. Grandin. (Courtesy of Church History Library.)

injustice and abuses, Church leaders welcomed the opportunity to form a battalion. Although unaware to the Mormon rank and file, Brigham Young had strategically sent agents east seeking federal assistance in relocating to the West. Despite reservations like those expressed by Stout, roughly five hundred men enlisted at the urging of Church leaders. In the end, the volunteer group marched nearly two thousand grueling miles from Council Bluffs to San Diego through some of the most unforgiving and arid terrain in North America. While the Battalion never participated in any combat, their list of accomplishments included establishing new wagon routes to the Pacific and helping to secure California for the expansion of the United States. A few discharged members of the Battalion were present when James Marshall discovered gold in the American River at Coloma on January 24, 1848, an event that marked the beginning of the historic California Gold Rush. Countless hopeful miners came from around the world, and gold seekers by the tens of thousands hustled overland to the goldfields, making use of trails blazed by Battalion members headed east to reunite with the main body of the Church.

Within the larger context of the Mexican War, this religion-based U.S. military battalion was a minor participant. However, the march from Council Bluffs to the Pacific by these mostly young Mormon soldiers forever changed and broadened their world view. The collective experience and maturity they gained during their enlistment would bless the Church they loved in countless ways for the rest of their lives. Many became colonizers, missionaries, and leaders in communities throughout the American West, even in the South Pacific and Mexico.

To understand the motivation and faith of the members of the Mormon Battalion, one must understand what led up to their enlistment in the summer of 1846. Their story really began in 1820 in upstate New York with Joseph Smith, a fourteen-year-old farm boy earnestly seeking answers to religious questions as well as his personal standing before God. He became concerned for his soul "at about the age of twelve" in the highly charged religious climate of the Second Great Awakening.[4] The confusion caused by contending preachers compelled young Smith to seek answers in the Bible. A passage in the book of James prompted him to retreat to a nearby grove of trees and approach the Lord in prayer to "obtain mercy" and "to know which of all the sects was right." He later recounted, "A piller of light above the brightness of the sun at noon day come down from above and rested upon me and I was filled with the spirit of god and the Lord opened the heavens upon me and I saw the Lord and he spake unto me saying Joseph my son thy sins are forgiven thee."[5] Joseph was instructed by God the Father and Jesus Christ to join no church and was told that "the fullness of the gospel should at some future time be made known unto me."[6]

This epiphany was the first of many visions and revelations received by Joseph Smith during his short lifetime. In September 1823, an ancient prophet named Moroni appeared to Joseph and instructed him to go to a hill near his home in Manchester Township, New York, where some gold plates had been buried centuries previous. The plates contained a record of a civilization that had inhabited the American continent more than a millennia earlier. Smith obediently visited the hill every September for the next four years until Moroni entrusted him with the plates in 1827. Repeated attempts by others to steal the plates and threats of violence by locals persuaded Smith to leave New York for Harmony, Pennsylvania. Joseph did little by way of translation of the record until a prosperous farmer named Martin Harris became involved. Harris owned land north of Palmyra and desired to act as Joseph's scribe after "the Lord appeared unto him in a vision and shewed unto him his marvelous work which he was about to do."[7] By mid-June 1828, the two had completed a 116-page manuscript, and Harris pressured Joseph to allow him to borrow the pages and return to Palmyra in hopes of convincing his wife and friends of the book's divine origin and purpose. Despite being denied by the Lord twice, Harris persuaded Joseph to supplicate the Lord a third time. Harris was finally permitted to take the manuscript, which he subsequently lost, resulting in the plates being taken from Joseph for a season and Harris losing his position as scribe.

Following what Joseph described as "much humility and affliction of Soul," the plates were returned. With the assistance of several scribes, the work of translation moved slowly until Oliver Cowdery arrived in Harmony in April 1829. Cowdery was led to the Smith family by spiritual impressions, escorted to Harmony, and began scribing two days after meeting Joseph. Translation progressed at a rapid pace and through the "power of God" the translation was finished. The new volume of scripture, the Book of Mormon, was published on March 26, 1830; eleven days later, the Church of Christ (renamed The Church of Jesus Christ of Latter-day Saints in 1838) was organized in Fayette, New York, with roughly fifty people in attendance. [8]

Martin Harris (1783–1875) served as Joseph Smith's first scribe and helped finance the publication of the Book of Mormon. (Courtesy of Church History Library.)

Oliver Cowdery (1806–1850) was primary scribe of the Book of Mormon. (Courtesy of Church History Library.)

Image of Kirtland, Ohio, taken by George Edward Anderson in August 1907. The temple is visible on the bluff. (Courtesy of Church History Library.)

From the outset, the missionaries eagerly took the message of their new religion westward. While traveling to preach in western Missouri's Indian territory, a group of four missionaries taught a congregation in Kirtland, Ohio, led by a charismatic preacher named Sidney Rigdon. The group of more than one hundred converted within a few weeks and roughly doubled the size of the Church. In late December 1830, Joseph Smith, facing continued harassment in New York, appointed Kirtland by revelation as the new gathering place for the Church.[9] For the next seven years, Kirtland served as Church headquarters, during which time the Prophet Joseph Smith received numerous revelations and began a new translation of the Bible. Also under his direction, Church members constructed a temple and the community flourished. As the region's Mormon population swelled to a majority, difficulties with their neighbors increased. The national financial crisis of 1837 led to the closure of the Church-sponsored Kirtland Safety Society, financially devastating many Church members. Increasing dissension within the Church (partly from the bank failure), coupled with ongoing persecution, effectively ended the Church's presence in Kirtland. Joseph Smith left in January 1838, and many of the Saints joined their Prophet in Missouri in the months that followed.

Missouri served as a secondary gathering place in parallel with Kirtland throughout most of the 1830s. From the outset, Missourians did not receive the Saints warmly. Suspected Mormon abolitionist sentiment clashed with the slave culture practices of many Missourians. This, together with religious differences and a fear that the ever-increasing number of Mormons arriving in Missouri would soon control local politics and resources, created a volatile environment. Violence erupted, and the Saints were expelled from several counties before state legislators established Caldwell County as a location for Mormons to settle in 1836. However, hostility and confrontation continued to increase, finally culminating in the brutal murders of seventeen Mormons at Haun's Mill in the fall of 1838 and the infamous order issued by Governor Lilburn Boggs that called for the Mormons to "be exterminated or driven from the state." Missouri militias arrested a number of Church leaders, including Joseph Smith, on charges of treason. Joseph and his fellow Church leaders spent the next several months in prison. The conflict included the destruction of property and terrible atrocities, initiating the retreat of nearly ten thousand displaced Saints across the frozen Missouri terrain in the middle of winter under the direction of Apostle Brigham Young, where they mercifully found refuge across the Mississippi River in Quincy, Illinois.[10]

Joseph Smith escaped from prison in April 1839, rejoined the main body of the Church in Quincy, and rallied the disheartened Saints to commence building a settlement known as Commerce—soon renamed Nauvoo—on the banks of the Mississippi River. Land was purchased, swampy tracts were drained, and houses constructed. A steady stream of converts, including many from Europe, arrived in Nauvoo, bringing with them valuable skills and trades. New doctrines were received, a female Relief Society was organized, and construction of a temple began in 1841 at the sacrifice of Church members' time and commodities. Joseph did not live to see the temple completed, but rooms were dedicated and used for sacred ordinances as they were finished. By April 1846, finishing touches were made on the temple and it was publicly dedicated on May 1 by Orson Hyde.[11]

As had occurred previously in Ohio and Missouri, citizens in surrounding communities soon felt threatened by the Church's rapidly expanding presence and influence. Nauvoo's charter authorized a remarkable amount of autonomy that was common among other cities in Illinois at the time. The state had granted similar charters that provided for a municipal court system and city council, but the Nauvoo charter differed from others in the authority it granted to organize a city militia and university. Moreover, the booming population allowed for Nauvoo to control elections with the majority vote, and non-Mormons despised the lack of separation between church and state. Many of the city leaders served simultaneously as Church leaders and could protect the Church under the auspices of the charter.[12] Another point of contention centered around allegations of plural marriage being secretly practiced by Church leaders, which was largely responsible for the apostasy of a number of Smith's inner circle of associates and which intensified persecution. The situation boiled over in early June 1844 when Smith and the city

Daguerreotype of the Nauvoo Temple looking northwest, circa 1847. The temple was dedicated in 1846 and burned by arson fire in 1848. (Courtesy of Church History Library.)

Drawing of the Carthage Jail where Joseph and Hyrum Smith were murdered on June 27, 1844. (Courtesy of Church History Library.)

Brigham Young (1801–1877) and the vanguard company of Mormon pioneers left Winter Quarters in April 1847 and reached the Salt Lake Valley in July. (Courtesy of Church History Library.)

council ordered the removal of the Nauvoo Expositor, an anti-Mormon newspaper, following the publication of its inaugural issue. The destruction of the printing press led to Smith's arrest; within days, he and his brother Hyrum were murdered by a mob on June 27, 1844, while in jail in Carthage, Illinois.

The enemies of the Church presumed that Smith's death would put an end to Mormonism. With most of the members of the Quorum of the Twelve away on missions, a number of aspiring successors emerged. Confusion about who should succeed Joseph Smith as leader of the Church was rampant. By August 1844 most of the Twelve had returned to Nauvoo, and the majority of the Saints aligned with Brigham Young as senior member of the Quorum of the Twelve.

When the Church did not disappear after the death of Joseph and Hyrum, tensions in the region resumed, and plans for the Saints to leave Nauvoo were in full swing by the fall of 1845. Available maps and accounts of the exploration of Alta (or Upper) California were carefully studied, and Nauvoo was transformed into a bustling wagon factory. Great efforts were made to finish the temple so as many Latter-day Saints as possible might participate in sacred temple ordinances prior to crossing the plains. Their determination to complete the temple while fully aware that the magnificent structure would be abandoned illustrates the importance the Saints placed on receiving temple ordinances. From December 1845 to February 1846, Church members flocked to the temple to make solemn covenants with God prior to departing for the West.

A number of retrospective accounts date Joseph Smith's prophecy of relocating to the Rocky Mountains as far back as the 1830s. Wilford Woodruff recalled that Smith prophesied that "this people will go into the Rocky Mountains."[13] However, questions regarding the Saints' final destination remained. At one time or another Texas, Alta California, Oregon Territory, and Vancouver Island were all considered viable options. Even as Brigham Young's vanguard company rolled out of Winter

Quarters in April 1847, contemporaneous sources indicate that Young either remained unsure of their precise destination or he was simply reluctant to disclose the information to keep the government and political foes in the dark.

The Saints began to vacate Nauvoo earlier than anticipated due to unrelenting mob violence as well as rumors that federal officials threatened to arrest members of the Twelve Apostles. The exodus occurred in three waves over the course of an eight-month period in 1846.[14] Rather than wait until springtime as initially planned, the first wave of evacuees began crossing the Mississippi into Iowa Territory on February 4. Leaving so early in the year put the group at a great disadvantage; they not only had to combat cold weather, but winter travel meant there would be no grass to feed their teams. Ezra T. Benson captured the feelings of the Saints when he recorded: "About the ninth of February [1846] I started with my two wives and two children in the dead of winter, leaving my pleasant home and fireside. I left my furniture standing in the house, such as chairs, tables, bedsteads and clock. When we left, Bro. Porters' family took possession of the house and the things which were in it. We crossed the Mississippi River, leaving our beautiful city and temple, not knowing where we should go."[15]

Daguerreotype of Ezra T. Benson (1811–1869), circa 1850s. Benson was called to the Quorum of the Twelve Apostles on July 16, 1846, the same day that the Mormon Battalion was officially enlisted into the U.S. Army. (Courtesy of Church History Library.)

Brigham Young organized the "Camp of Israel" into companies of tens, fifties, and hundreds shortly after they set out across Iowa. Initial indecision on which route to follow, lack of provisions, illness, and harsh weather all contributed to a miserable and prolonged trek across Iowa for the initial wave of pioneer companies. Along the way roads and bridges were improved and two temporary settlements were established within thirty miles of each other as way stations for approaching Saints. The first of these, Garden Grove, was located about 150 miles west of Nauvoo and provided food and shelter for destitute Saints. A second settlement was located on the Grand River for the same purpose and was named Mount Pisgah by Parley P. Pratt. Those who lacked teams and supplies remained in these settlements to cultivate the land and construct additional dwellings for incoming emigrants.

Brigham Young and his advance company pushed onto the Missouri River, reaching Council Bluffs on June 14. At this point, Young was still optimistic about a core group reaching the Rockies and preparing their newfound Zion for the influx of Saints the following year. Still, the circumstances of the Saints were so straitened that any hope of continuing to the Rockies in 1846 became increasingly

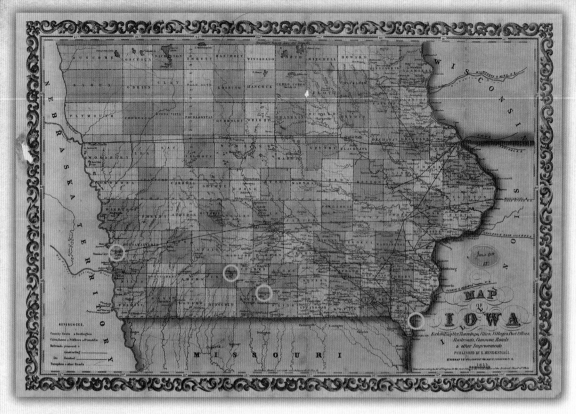

1855 map of Iowa with the locations of Nauvoo, Garden Grove, Mount Pisgah, and Council Bluffs inserted. (Courtesy of the Library of Congress.)

unrealistic. With the U.S. government request to enlist five hundred Mormon men in the war with Mexico, any hope of making it west evaporated.[16] Colonel Stephen Watts Kearny received orders from Secretary of War William Marcy on June 3, authorizing Kearny to approach the "large body of Mormon emigrants" to muster them into military service to assist in the war with Mexico.[17]

When Captain James Allen and his small contingent of US soldiers rode into Mormon camps in mid-June 1846 to recruit a battalion, they initially received a cold reception from many of the Saints. To the rank and file, the U.S. government's request that hundreds abandon their families in the name of a country that had repeatedly failed to defend and uphold their fundamental rights despite desperate pleadings seemed reprehensible. Yet they heeded the call of Brigham Young and became the only known military unit in American history mustered into service based on religious affiliation.[18] The unit served for one year (July 1846 to July 1847) before being discharged. Along the nearly two-thousand-mile trek, command of the Mormon Battalion changed several times. Nearly all of the large contingent of women and children that accompanied the Battalion were detached to Pueblo in present-day Colorado along with soldiers too sick to continue. The soldiers endured privation, thirst, and a litany of other hardships during the seemingly ceaseless march to the Pacific, and a struggle between military and ecclesiastical authority for the unit's loyalty simmered and occasionally boiled over during the long march.

The following chapters divide the march into four segments: Council Bluffs to Fort Leavenworth, Fort Leavenworth to Santa Fe, Santa Fe to the Pima villages, and the Pima villages to the Pacific. The compelling story of the Mormon Battalion centers on its remarkable march across half a continent. In facing their obstacles and persevering, the soldiers of the Mormon Battalion accomplished their stated military objective—creating a viable wagon road to the Pacific. In countless ways, their accomplishment changed their lives forever. Along with their deep faith, the year of military service taught them that they could shape their own future. Their religion taught them that with faith, their lives could be full of possibilities. Their military service reinforced that faith and strengthened their belief in themselves and what they could do with their lives. In short, it transformed their view of the world and their place in it. Their display of determination, endurance, and sacrifice embodies the romance of frontier America and the westward expansion of the nineteenth century.

Endnotes

1   Initial plans to depart in the spring appeared in an October 8, 1845, circular published in *Times and Seasons* 6 (November 1, 1845). The decision to move up the departure date occurred on January 11, 1846. See also Elden J. Watson, ed., *Manuscript History of Brigham Young, 1846–1847* (Salt Lake City: Elden J. Watson, 1971), 10.

2   Benjamin Chamberlain Critchlow, Autobiography, 3, Church History Library, The Church of Jesus Christ of Latter-day Saints, Salt Lake City, Utah (hereinafter cited as Church History Library).

3   Hosea Stout, Journal, 28 June 1846, Church History Library.

4   Joseph Smith, 1832 history, in Dean C. Jessee, ed., *Personal Writings of Joseph Smith* (Salt Lake City: Deseret Book, 2002), 10.

5   Joseph Smith, 1832 history, 11.

6   Joseph Smith, Historical Sketch, March 1, 1842, in Jessee, *Personal Writings of Joseph Smith*, 242.

7   Joseph Smith, 1832 history, 13.

8   Joseph Smith, Historical Sketch, in Jessee, 243; Richard L. Bushman, *Joseph Smith and the Beginnings of Mormonism* (Champaign, IL: University of Illinois Press, 1985), 143.

9   Doctrine and Covenants 37:3.

10 See Alexander L. Baugh, *A Call to Arms: 1838 Mormon Defense of Northern Missouri* (Ph.D. dissertation, Brigham Young University, 1996).

11 Wilford Woodruff, Journal, 1 May 1846, in Scott G. Kenney, ed., *Wilford Woodruff's Journal, 1833–1898*, 9 vols. (Midvale, UT: Signature Books, 1983), 3:42.

12 Glen M. Leonard, *Nauvoo: A Place of Peace, A People of Promise* (Salt Lake City: Deseret Book Co. and Brigham Young University Press, 2002), 99–105.

13 Wilford Woodruff, *Conference Report*, April 1898. For additional accounts of Joseph Smith's prophecy of the Saints relocating to the Rocky Mountains, see Affidavit of Paulina E. Phelps Lyman before James Jack, Salt Lake City, July 31, 1902, Church History Library; and *Journal of Discourses*, 26 vols. (Liverpool: S. W. Richards et al., 1854–1886), 3:257–258, 4:41, 11:16.

14 William G. Hartley, "The Pioneer Trek: Nauvoo to Winter Quarters," *Ensign* 27, no. 6 (June 1997), 32–34.

15 Ezra T. Benson, "An Autobiography," *Instructor* 80, no. 2 (May 1945), 215.

16 James Emmett took a group of Latter-day Saints across Iowa Territory in 1844 and reached Camp Vermillion in present-day South Dakota. George Miller was assigned to lead an advance company in June 1846 to Fort Laramie in preparation for the main body of the Saints to move west. Both the Miller and Emmett companies eventually merged and wintered in a Ponca Indian village in northeast Nebraska. For more on the Emmett-Miller companies, see William G. Hartley, *My Best For the Kingdom: History and Autobiography of John Lowe Butler, a Mormon Frontiersman* (Salt Lake City: Aspen Books, 1993).

17 Marcy to Kearny, June 3, 1846, House Exec. Doc., as quoted in David L. Bigler and Will Bagley, eds., *Army of Israel: Mormon Battalion Narratives*, Kingdom of the West: The Mormons and the American Frontier Series, vol. 4 (Spokane, WA: The Arthur H. Clark Company, 2000), 38; and Richard E. Bennett, *Mormons at the Missouri: Winter Quarters, 1846–1852* (Norman: University of Oklahoma Press, 1987). Colonel Stephen Watts Kearny was promoted to the rank of general on June 30, 1846.

18 Fleek, *History May Be Searched in Vain*, 134–135.

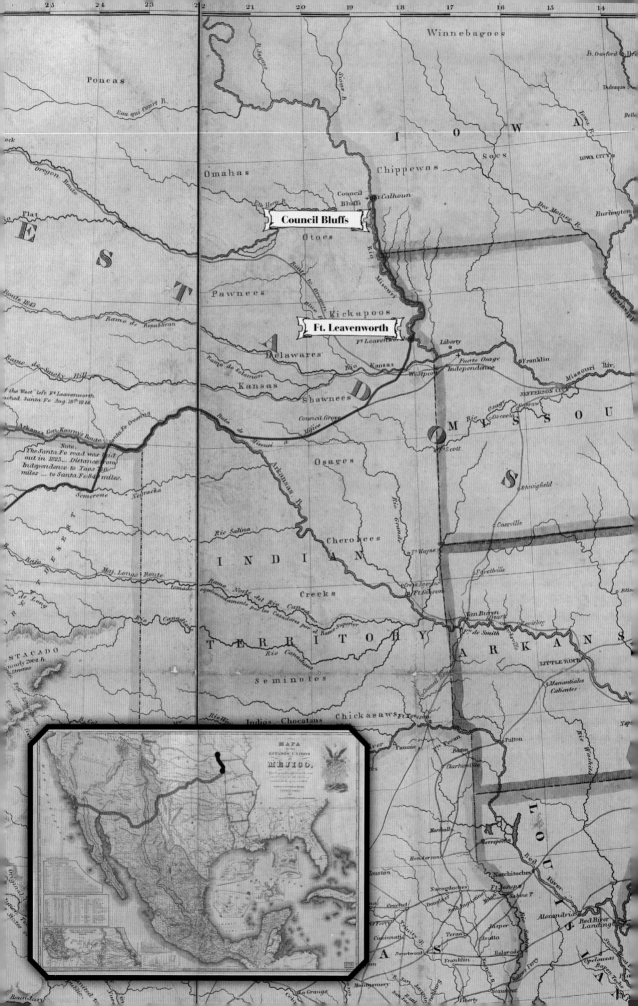

Council Bluffs

Ft. Leavenworth

Chapter Two

ENLISTMENT & DEPARTURE

"Quite a hard pill to swallow"

On January 20, 1846, two weeks before the first company left Nauvoo and crossed the Mississippi River, the High Council deliberated over options for financing the move west. The group determined to dispatch an advance company to plant crops in the Rocky Mountains and issued a circular stating in part:

In the event of the president's recommendations to build block houses and stockade forts on the route to Oregon, becoming a law, we have encouragement of having that work to do: and under our peculiar circumstances, we can do it with less expense to the government than any other people.

We also further declare for the satisfaction of some who have concluded that our grievances have alienated us from our country, that our patriotism has not been overcome by fire—by sword—by daylight, nor by midnight assassinations, which we have endured; neither have they alienated us from the institutions of our country. Should hostilities arise between the government of the United

"A Circular of the High Council," *Times and Seasons* 6, no. 21, January 20, 1846. This circular was addressed to Church members announcing plans for departing from Nauvoo earlier than anticipated. (Courtesy of Church History Library.)

States and any other power, in relation to the right of possessing the territory of Oregon, we are on hand to sustain the claims of the United States government to that country. It is geographically ours; and of right, no foreign power should hold dominion there: and if our services are required to prevent it, those services will be cheerfully rendered according to our ability.[1]

Six days later a letter was sent to Brigham Young's nephew, Jesse C. Little, asking that he oversee the Eastern States Mission of the Church. Before leaving Nauvoo, Little received the additional assignment to approach government leaders in Washington, DC, asking for their help in the move west. If during his visit "our government shall offer any facilities for emigrating to the western coast, embrace those facilities, if possible. As a wise and faithful man, take every honorable advantage of the times you can." Little later explained to Brigham Young that he "felt an anxious desire for the deliverance of the saints, and resolved upon visiting James K. Polk, president of the United States, to lay the situation of my persecuted brethren before him, and ask him, as the representative of our country, to stretch forth the federal arm in their behalf."[2]

Jesse C. Little (1815–1893) met with officials in Washington, DC, by assignment from his uncle, Brigham Young, in an attempt to obtain financial assistance for the move west. (Courtesy of Church History Library.)

While in Philadelphia preaching at a church meeting, Little met twenty-four-year-old Thomas L. Kane. This providential encounter had a great impact on the Latter-day Saints, as Kane became a strong advocate for the Mormons in the years ahead. The son of a federal judge and well connected in political circles, Kane was intrigued by the Mormons and struck up conversation with Little following the meeting. The two spent the next week discussing the westward movement of the Saints and national politics. By the end of the week, Kane penned a letter of introduction for Little to deliver to Vice-President George M. Dallas. The strategic note indirectly warned Dallas of the possibility of the Mormons becoming disloyal to the United States and aligning themselves with foreign powers.[3] Undoubtedly, the contents would be discussed with Dallas's associates and catch the attention of President James K. Polk.

In order to arrange a meeting with President Polk, Little solicited letters of introduction from a number of prominent individuals, including Vice-President Dallas; New Hampshire Governor John H. Steele; New York businessman Alfred G. Benson; and Amos Kendall, former Postmaster General and close friend of Polk.[4] Little arrived in Washington, DC, on May

21, just eight days after Polk declared war on Mexico. The conflict was sparked by a dispute between the United States and Mexico, with Mexico claiming the border was the Nueces River and the United States insisting it was the Rio Grande River. However, the disputed boundary itself was the result of much deeper issues that culminated in the Mexican-American War. In reality, a combination of social, cultural, racial, religious, and economic factors that fueled an American expansionist vision led to the outbreak of the war. Known as Manifest Destiny, a term attributed to editor John L. O'Sullivan of the *Democratic Review*, the phrase embodied the belief that the United States was destined to expand and encompass the land between the Atlantic and Pacific oceans. Polk was a strong advocate of stretching the nation's borders to include what was then termed Alta California, an area spanning most of the American West.

The Polk administration's hope that the Mexican War would end quickly were soon dashed. Although they lacked seasoned political and military leadership and were hampered by inadequate training and supplies, the Mexicans fought tenaciously for their homeland. It became a bloody and costly conflict for both sides. The Mormon Battalion, always on the periphery of the conflict, never engaged in the horrific and bloody battles that took place in the heart of Mexico. In relation to the totality of the conflict, the military contribution of the Battalion was minimal. Understandably, descendants of Battalion soldiers as well as many other Latter-day Saints have focused almost entirely on the march, showing little interest in the context of the larger conflict.

Some may question why historians of the Mexican War have paid scant attention to the remarkable march and subsequent accomplishments of the Mormon Battalion in California. Part of the answer may be one of scale. While tens of thousands of casualties were occurring on both the American and Mexican sides of the skirmish, the single battalion of Mormons numbering no more than five hundred men never truly became a factor in the war's outcome. Fortunate in their timing, they consistently arrived too late to be involved in any combat. For example, as the tail of Kearny's Army of the West, the Mormon Battalion arrived a couple weeks after Kearny's brutal fight at San Pascual, where his men tragically suffered 30 percent casualties and may have been annihilated without the arrival of Commodore Robert F. Stockton's reinforcements. In contrast to the war experience of the Mormon Battalion, American regiments led by the likes of Zachary Taylor, John Wool, Winfield Scott, and Alexander Doniphan were forced to penetrate deep into the heart of Mexico, where thousands of American soldiers died

Daguerreotype of U.S. President James K. Polk (1795–1849) taken in 1849 shortly before his death. Polk authorized Colonel Stephen W. Kearny to recruit "a few hundred of the Mormons" to fight in the Mexican War. (Courtesy of the Library of Congress.)

Opposite Bottom: Thomas L. Kane (1822–1883), a compassionate friend to the Mormons, assisted Jesse C. Little in Washington, DC, visited Council Bluffs during the recruitment of the Mormon Battalion, and helped negotiate a peaceful settlement to the Utah War in 1858. (Courtesy of the Library of Congress.)

from disease or in combat. Aside from the human cost, the United States spent more than two billion dollars (adjusted to present-day values) in prosecuting the war.[5]

The timing of Jesse Little, who arrived just prior to the declaration of war, became a significant factor in the creation of the Mormon Battalion. He met with Amos Kendall over the course of a week, and their discussions served as the genesis of the plan to enlist Mormons and station them in Alta California. Fearing that he had little time to persuade Polk to assist the Saints in their move west, on June 1 Little penned an aggressive letter interlaced with subtle threats. After recalling the persecutions endured by these "true hearted Americans" and reassuring Polk of the upstanding character of his people, the letter informed the president that the Mormons were headed "over the Prairies and Rocky Mountains to find a new home in the howling wilderness" and they desired the assistance of the United States government. Little inflated the numbers of Saints gathering to the west, warning that "we would disdain to receive assistance from a foreign power . . . unless our government shall turn us off in this great crisis and will not help us, but compel us to be foreigners." If the president refused to help in the Mormon cause, Little threatened to "cross the trackless ocean" and negotiate with rival foreign governments.[6]

Little's impassioned letter produced its intended effect, and Polk worried that, in a time of war, the Mormons might pose a serious risk in the dispute over Oregon Country and Alta California.[7] In discussing war stratagem on June 2 with his cabinet, Polk decided to send a military expedition to California under the leadership of Colonel Stephen Watts Kearny. Kearny was authorized "to receive into service as volunteers a few hundred of the Mormons who are now on their way to California, with a view to conciliate them, attach them to our country, & prevent them from taking part against us."[8] The following day Little was assured by Polk himself that he had no biases toward the Mormons and they "would be treated as all other American citizens were." Polk then "told Mr. Little that we were at War with Mexico, and asked him if 500 or more of the mormons now on their way to California would be willing on their arrival to that country to volunteer and enter the U.S. army in that war." Little quickly consented and offered to set out immediately to locate Church leaders in Iowa Territory and make the necessary arrangements. In his diary, Polk privately restated his primary purpose for issuing the call for the Battalion: "The mormons, if taken into the service, will constitute not more than ¼ of Col. Kearney's [sic] command, and the main objective of taking them

Colonel Stephen Watts Kearny (1794–1848) was appointed by President James K. Polk to lead a military expedition during the Mexican War to secure the trade route in New Mexico and occupy Alta California. (Courtesy of Bancroft Library.)

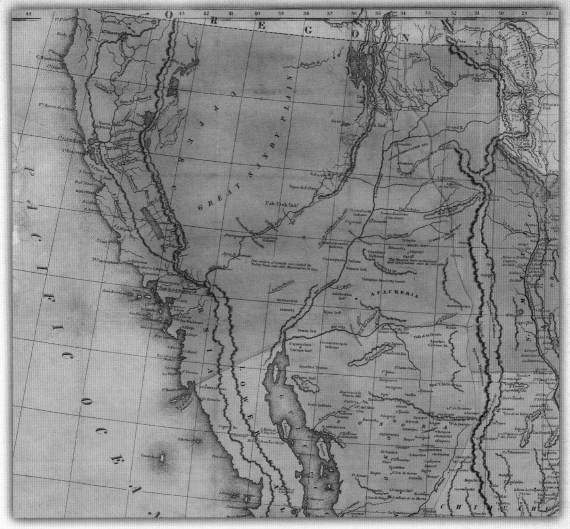

into service would be to conciliate them, and prevent them from assuming a hostile attitude toward the U.S. after their arrival in California."[9]

The term *California* had a different meaning in 1846, and the boundaries of California were drastically different at the time of the Mexican War than they are now. Alta (or Upper) California comprised the massive northern portion of Mexico, comprising nearly six hundred thousand square miles and including present-day California, Nevada, Arizona, Utah, western Colorado, and southwestern Wyoming. Baja (or Lower) California referred to the peninsula west of mainland Mexico. Alta California became American soil at the end of the Mexican War with the signing of the Treaty of Guadalupe Hidalgo on February 2, 1848.

Secretary of War William Marcy relayed a slightly modified version of Polk's directives to Kearny at Fort Leavenworth, calling for the organization of an army to strike out overland to Santa Fe, retain control of the trade route in Nuevo México, and occupy Alta California. Kearny received his orders on June 3 and subsequently instructed Captain James Allen to travel north to the Mormon

This 1847 H. S. Tanner map shows the nearly six hundred thousand square miles that comprised Alta (or Upper) California. This land was ceded to the United States at the end of the Mexican War with the signing of the Treaty of Guadalupe Hidalgo on February 2, 1848. (Courtesy of Church History Library.)

camps in Iowa Territory and enlist a battalion. Allen's orders read in part:

> There is a large body of Mormons who are desirous of emigrating to California, for the purpose of settling in that country, and I have, therefore, to direct that you will proceed to their camps and endeavor to raise from among them four or five companies of volunteers to join me in my expedition to that country. . . . The companies, after being organized, will be marched to this post, where they will be armed and prepared for the field, after which they will, under your command, follow on my trail in the direction of Santa Fe, and where you will receive further orders from me . . . . I cannot doubt but that you will, in a few days, be able to raise five hundred young and efficient men for this expedition.[10]

Wilford Woodruff (1807–1898) was among the first group of Mormons contacted by Captain James Allen. Woodruff believed Allen and his escorts to be spies sent by the U.S. Government to observe the movements of the Saints. (Courtesy of Church History Library.)

Allen received his orders on June 19 and made his first contact with the Mormons seven days later in Mount Pisgah, where he met with William Huntington, leader of the Saints in Pisgah, and apostle Wilford Woodruff, who happened to be passing through when Allen and his entourage arrived. Huntington permitted Allen to address Church members. Woodruff noted, "I had some reason to believe them to be spies and that the president had no hand in it. We however treated them with civility & directed them on to Council Bluffs to lay the case before the President."[11] Woodruff immediately dispatched an express rider to deliver a letter to Brigham Young regarding Allen and his intended purpose.

Allen was not well received by the Mount Pisgah Saints. Many, like Woodruff, were suspicious of his motives, thinking he was sent to spy on them in response to a fictitious claim that the Mormons intended to unite with the Indians and to declare war on the United States. Brigham Young and the initial company of Saints had arrived at the Missouri River on June 14, less than two weeks prior to Allen's appearance at Pisgah. Within two days, word of Allen and "officers of the United States Army . . . with a requisition from the President . . . for 500 soldiers to march to Santa Fe against Mexico & from thence to California" reached Church leaders in Council Bluffs.[12]

One of Allen's first actions was to issue a circular to the Mormons, defining and explaining his visit:

Circular to the Mormons.

Mormons.

I have come among you instructed by Colonel S. W. Kearny of the U. S. Army, now commanding the "Army of the West" to visit the Mormon Camps and to accept the services, for twelve months of four or five companies of the Mormon Men who may be willing to serve their country for that period in our present war with Mexico — This force to unite with the Army of the West at Santa Fee and be marched thence to California, where they will be discharged.

They will receive pay and rations and other allowances such as other volunteer or regular soldiers receive, from the day they shall be mustered into the service and will be entitled to all the comforts and benefits of regular soldiers of the Army: and when discharged as contemp-ted, at California they will be given gratis, their arms and accoutrements, with which they will be fully equipped at Fort Leavenworth.

Thus is offered to the Mormon people

I have come among you ... to visit the Mormon camps, and to accept the service for twelve months, of four or five companies of Mormon men who may be willing to serve their country for that period in our present war with Mexico; this force to unite with the Army of the West at Santa Fe, and be marched thence to California, where they will be discharged.

They will receive pay and rations, and other allowances, such as volunteers or regular soldiers receive...."[13]

Captain James Allen's July 1846 circular to the Mormons requesting five hundred volunteers to serve in the Mexican War. (Courtesy of Church History Library.)

This circular made the rounds throughout Mormon settlements over the next few weeks while Allen attempted to recruit the necessary men to fill five companies.

Emotions ran high in the wake of the request, and many Church members were angered by the audacity of the government in expecting them to forsake their families and church at such a vulnerable time. William Clayton recorded, "the feeling amongst the brethren is that they are spies sent to learn our movements and watch us. It is evident the U.S. are afraid of us and perhaps the serpent will send a flood after us but the earth will help us."[14] Albert Smith poignantly described the feelings of many: "For the government to mak[e] Such a demand when we ware driven from our homes & Posses[s]ions & ware scattred upon the plains from Nauvoo to the Mosurie [Missouri] river was more Cruel than the Grave."[15]

Thomas L. Kane sketch of Council Bluffs, July 14, 1846. (Courtesy of L. Tom Perry Special Collections, Brigham Young University.)

Clearly, this was no trivial appeal to those strewn across the Iowa Territory. It would have been an immense sacrifice even in ideal circumstances. To many Latter-day Saints—exposed to the elements, living in a state of homelessness, and battling ill health—it seemed virtually impossible. The initial reaction of the Mormon rank and file must have been discouraging to Allen, who was expected to return to Fort Leavenworth in a matter of days with five hundred recruits.

Captain Allen made the 160-mile trip west to Council Bluffs, arriving the evening of June 30; there he arranged a meeting with Brigham Young and other Church leaders for the following morning. Seeing it as an opportunity to help the Church, President Young became the strongest advocate for the recruitment of the Battalion. However, even with President Young's assistance, it took Allen two and a half weeks to enlist enough men to fill five companies. Without President Young's endorsement, coupled with his inspiring pleas to the men of the various camps, Allen would have returned to Leavenworth empty-handed. As historian Sherman Fleek observed, "There is no doubt that without Brigham Young's acceptance of the offer to form the battalion, there would have been no Mormon Battalion."[16] Captain Allen acknowledged the effect

Brigham Young and Church leaders had on recruitment, stating that he felt "much indebted for their active and zealous exertions to raise the volunteer force that I was authorized to ask for."[17] It may have surprised many Church members to see Brigham Young embrace the government's plan to recruit five hundred Mormons so quickly. Most of the Saints were not privy to Brigham Young's role in initiating the process to seek government work contracts six months earlier by sending Jesse C. Little to the nation's capital.

Shortly before noon on July 1, Brigham Young introduced Captain Allen, who addressed the Saints and explained that he was sent under the orders of Colonel Kearny—General Kearny as of June 30—to recruit five hundred Mormons to assist in the Mexican War. Their unit would comprise a small component of thousands of volunteers drawn from among several states. Kearny's orders were rehearsed along with the circular issued at Mount Pisgah a few days earlier. At noon Brigham Young addressed the group, instructing "the brethren to make a distinction between this action of the general government, and their former oppressions in Missouri and Illinois." He reasoned with the Saints and endorsed the raising of a battalion, stating his desire that they be the first to "set their feet on the soil of California." The men were assured that their families would be cared for in their absence and that Brigham Young himself would "do my best to see all their families brought forward, so far as my influence can be extended and feed them when I had anything to eat myself."[18]

The recruiting campaign next turned eastward to the Mormon settlements of Mount Pisgah and Garden Grove. The campaign was preceded by a letter in which Brigham Young reassured Church members of the army's intentions:

Brigham Young, pictured here in 1850, accompanied Captain James Allen to visit Mormon camps and was instrumental in the recruitment of the nearly five hundred men that comprised the Mormon Battalion. (Courtesy of Church History Library.)

> Elder Little . . . has been to see the president [Polk] on the subject of emigrating the saints to the western coast, and confirms all that Captain Allen has stated to us. The United States want our friendship, the president wants to do us good and secure our confidence. The outfit of this five hundred men costs us nothing and their pay will be sufficient to take their families over the mountains. There is war between Mexico and the United States, to whom California must fall a prey, and if we are the first settlers, the old citizens cannot have a Hancock or Missouri pretext to mob the saints. The thing is from above, for our good, has long been understood between us and the United

States government. . . . The church could not help the twelve over the mountains, when they wanted to go, and now we will help the churches.[19]

Although Brigham Young's encouragement and approval of the raising of a battalion certainly softened resistance and induced many to enlist, it did not always diminish negative feelings. Henry W. Bigler recorded, "It was against my feelings and against the feelings of my brethren although we were willing to obey counsel believing all things would work for the best in the end. Still it looked hard when we called to mind the mobbings and drivings, the killing of our leaders, the burning of our homes and forcing us to leave the States and Uncle Sam take no notice of it and then to call on us to help fight his battles to me it was an insult."[20]

For others, attitudes changed based on their faith that Brigham Young was conveying the will of the Lord. William Hyde later wrote, "When the news [of the call of the Battalion] came, I looked upon my family and then upon my aged parents, and upon the situation of the camps in the midst of an uncultivated wild, Indian country, and my soul revolted. But when I came to learn the mind of the Lord, and on learning that the offering had to be made— and when our beloved president came to know who among the people were ready to be offered for the cause, I said: 'Here am I, take me.'"[21]

Many, like Samuel H. Rogers, considered enlistment in the Battalion as a sacrifice to accomplish the greater good. He stated, "it was like a ram caught in a thicket and that it would be better to sacrifice the ram than to have Isaac die. Reflecting upon the subject, it came to my mind that Isaac, in the figure, represented the church . . . and for the saving of its life I was willing to go on this expedition."[22]

In addition to Captain Allen, Thomas L. Kane also arrived in Council Bluffs on July 11. Having helped Jesse Little gain an audience with President Polk a few months earlier, Kane desired to join the Mormon camps in Iowa to satisfy both his "personal ambition and humanitarian sentiment."[23] Initially desiring to promote himself by writing a compelling book about his experience among the Mormons and a journey to California, Kane was quickly filled with empathy for the peculiar band of refugees, and from that time forward he always assisted them whenever possible. He in turn made an immediate impression among the Mormons. Wilford Woodruff felt Kane possessed "the spirit of a Gentleman" with "much interest in our welfare" and "from the information we recieved from him we were convinced that God had began to move upon the heart of the President [Polk] And others in this Nation to begin to act for our interest And the general good of Zion."[24]

William Hyde (1818–1874) was a member of Company B, and like many he struggled with the decision to enlist in the Mormon Battalion; his decisio to enlist required Hyde to abandon his family in the midst of the trek west. (Courtesy of Church History

While visiting the Saints, Kane became deathly ill and was nursed back to health by Church members. He never forgot that kindness, and it undoubtedly strengthened his resolve to defend and assist the Mormons in the years ahead.

Returning to Council Bluffs, Brigham Young assembled a large meeting on July 13 centered on the sending off of the Battalion. The first four companies were organized with Jefferson Hunt, Jesse D. Hunter, James Brown, and Nelson Higgins nominated as captains by Young and the Quorum of the Twelve. This mode of selecting captains contradicted the typical appointment of officers in a U.S. military unit and established from the outset that this unit was theocratic in nature. Rather than having the men elect their own officers, Brigham Young treated the appointment of the officers much as he would issue Church assignments or a mission call.

Brigham Young took advantage of his time with Allen and secured a number of promises. The most important was the granting of permission for the Mormons to "reside for a time" on Pottawattami Indian lands on the western banks of the Missouri River, where Winter Quarters was established in September 1846.[25] While Allen may have lacked the authority to make such a promise, it was good enough for Brigham Young, who desired to establish Winter Quarters on the west side of the Missouri River. Allen further promised not to divide the men and promised that Jefferson Hunt would assume leadership of the Mormon Battalion if Allen received a change of command or for other reasons, such as illness, could no longer remain in command.[26]

On July 16, the recruits at Council Bluffs, comprising four full companies and part of a fifth, gathered in the square to officially enlist in the United States military for a period of one year. An American flag was hoisted in a tree, the oath of office was read by Captain Allen, and the men were sworn in as volunteers in the United States Army. Shortly following the ceremony, the first orders were issued, officially declaring that with the formation of the Mormon Battalion, Captain James Allen was now Lieutenant Colonel Allen, and that they should be "held in readiness to march at the shortest notice, and as soon as the fifth company be filled all will be ready for movement." The Battalion staff and an assistant surgeon were appointed. Then the Battalion "marched 8 miles to the Missouri river, near a trading post kept by a Frenchman by the name of Sarpee [Sarpy]," where they were issued provisions.[27] After witnessing the Battalion march south, Wilford Woodruff wrote, "while casting my eyes upon them I considerd I was viewing the first Battalion of the Army of Israel . . . going to lay the foundation of A far greater work even preparing the way for the building of Zion."[28] After arriving at the trading post, many of the men returned to Council Bluffs to spend a few more cherished days with family and friends.

On July 18, along the banks of the Missouri, Brigham Young, Heber C. Kimball, Willard Richards, John Taylor, Parley P. Pratt, and Wilford Woodruff met privately with the Battalion; William Hyde recorded that they "gave us their last charge and blessing, with a firm promise that on condition of faithfulness on our part, our lives should be spared and our expedition result in great good, and our names handed down in honorable remembrance to all generations."[29] Young took the opportunity to instruct the captains "to be fathers to their companies and manage their affairs by the power and influence of their priesthood; then they would have power to preserve their lives and the lives of their companies and escape difficulties. Pres Young told them he would not be afraid to pledge his right hand that every man will return alive, if they will perform their duties faithfully, without murmuring, and go in the name of the Lord, be humble and pray every morning and evening in their tents . . . , keep neat and clean, teach chastity, gentility, and civility; swearing must not be admitted, insult no man; have no contentious conversation with [any] people. . . . Should the battalion engage with the enemy and be successful, treat prisoners with the greatest civility, and never take life, if it can be avoided."[30] He further elaborated on the future designs of the Church. This was no ordinary military unit. In their eyes, Brigham Young's directions stemmed from a divine source and unquestionably superseded any military authority regardless of commission or rank. Tension between the religious and military lines of authority surfaced throughout the duration of the march to the Pacific.

Brigham Young further "assured the brethren that they would have no fighting to do; told them the Saints should go into the Great Basin, which was the place to build Temples; and where their strongholds should be against the mobs." Finally, he predicted that "the battalion would probably be disbanded about eight hundred miles from the place where the body of the Church should locate."[31]

A grand farewell ball was held on July 18 in a newly constructed bowery. William Pitt's brass band played "to the canto of debonair violins, the cheer of horns, the jingle of sleigh bells, and the jovial snoring of the tambourine, they did dance! . . . Light hearts, lithe figures, and light feet, had it their own way from an early hour till after the sun had dipped behind the sharp sky-line of the Omaha hills."[32] As the festivities wound down, Kane recorded the depth of emotions among the Saints when a young lady sang a final piece that brought many to tears.

The first four companies departed Council Bluffs on July 20 under the command of Allen. Tears ran freely throughout camp and "we took up the line of March for Fort Leavenworth, 200 miles distant, the men keeping time to 'The Girl I Left Behind Me.' It was a solemn time with us as we were leaving families and friends and near and dear relatives, not knowing how long we should be absent, and perhaps we might never see them again in this life. I bid my folks farewell and did not see them again for 9 years."[33]

Great effort went into raising enough volunteers to round out Company E and complete the five hundred Captain Allen needed. This fifth and final company left Council Bluffs on July 22 with Daniel C. Davis as their captain. The age of the men that comprised the Mormon Battalion's five companies spanned from fourteen to sixty-seven.[34] With an average age of twenty-seven, the majority were young men embarking on an adventure unlike anything they had ever experienced. Adding to the size of the group were family members of a number of the men who had received permission from Allen for their families to accompany them. At least thirty-four women and forty-four children traveled with the group to Fort Leavenworth. Most of these family members were detached from the Battalion in and around Santa Fe. The day before arriving in Fort Leavenworth, Lieutenant Colonel Allen compiled the first official roster of the Battalion; that roster listed twenty-two officers and four hundred and seventy-four enlisted volunteers, for a total of four hundred ninety-six men in five companies.[35] Although a number of scholars have done excellent research in an effort to create a definitive roster, suffice it to say that the recruitment was not a seamless process during which five hundred men lined up, enlisted, and headed south in a synchronized march.

Joining the Mormon Battalion was a great sacrifice to all those faced with the reality of heading off to war amidst the mass migration of the entire Church to an undetermined spot in Alta California, far to the west. Battalion soldiers captured the vivid and heart-wrenching scene of departure in their diaries. Zadok Judd wrote: "This was quite a hard pill to swallow—to leave wives and

A farewell ball was held for the departing soldiers and their families in Council Bluffs on July 18, 1846. (Courtesy of Church History Museum.)

children on the wild prairie, destitute and almost helpless, having nothing to rely on only the kindness of neighbors, and go to fight the battles of a government that had allowed some of its citizens to drive us from our homes, but the word came from the right source and seemed to bring the spirit of conviction of its truth with it and there was quite a number of company volunteered, myself and brother among them."[36]

Judd took comfort in his faith that Brigham Young was led by God. It pained him to leave his family at the mercy of neighbors who had families and concerns of their own. The separation was untimely, to say the least. Leaving one's family in the safety and comfort of their own home was tough enough, but to carry the added stress of abandoning them in the prairie more than a thousand miles short of their destination in the Rocky Mountains was a sacrifice almost too hard to bear. James S. Brown declared that he did "not suppose there is an individual in the Battalion, who, had he been left to his own thoughts and feelings, independent of counsel, would have enlisted. I would have felt very reluctant under the circumstances had it not been for the counsel of my brethren whom God authorized to dictate the affairs of His kingdom."[37]

George Washington Taggart (1816–1893) was a member of Company B. He was among the group of Battalion veterans that proceeded from the Salt Lake Valley to Winter Quarters in late 1847 to reunite with their families. (Courtesy of Church History Library.)

At the time George Washington Taggart enlisted in Company B, he had not seen his family for five months. He wrote a poignant letter to his sister explaining his decision to join the cause: "My faith is that you wil not murmur at My volunteering to absent myself from you for so long inasmuch as I go by council of the church, you may be assured Fanny it is a great disappointment and a wound to My natural feelings to tear Myself as it were away from My Family that I have not seen for five months . . . but I believe that the God of Israel will order all things right for those that act through a pure desire for the welfare of his Kingdom."[38]

William Hyde agonized over leaving his wife and two young children: "I returned to the camp where my family was situated, a distance of 8 miles. The thoughts of leaving them at this critical time are indescribable. Far from the land we had once called civilization, with no dwelling, save a wagon, with the scorching midsummer sun to beat upon them, with the prospect of the cold December blasts finding them in the same place. My family at this time consisted of a wife and two children, the eldest of whom was but three years and a half. And the situation of my wife was such as to cause her to require, if ever, the assistance and watch care of her companion . . . All had supposed their hands were full before the requisition was made; now they felt that there was placed upon them a threefold charge."[39]

Many could hardly bear watching their loved ones march away

with a few supplies hefted over their shoulders, blending into the horizon within a few minutes. No one was quite sure how long they might be separated or the perils of war they might encounter in a foreign land. Henry Standage grabbed his "knapsack and left the Camp of Israel, leaving my wife and mother in tears."[40] Adjutant George P. Dykes felt the need to repent for leaving his "aged Mother and a Family dearer than life in the wide spreading prearies with [nothing] more than their waggon &c for habitations."[41]

The opening days on the trail along the Missouri River to Fort Leavenworth brought extremely hot weather that tried the stamina of the group. Added to this, a shortage of food needed to sustain the large group tested the stamina of even the strongest. Whereas Allen was sympathetic and advocated moderate daily hikes in the less-than-ideal conditions, Adjutant Dykes insisted on an aggressive march, causing many to become ill. John Steele recorded: "I came to a cold spring of water and drank freely of it, my bowels being empty not eating much that day, it took hold and cramped my bowels and stomach and I was in exceeding pain; then the Elders laid hands on me and I got a little better so as to go along. The brethren stand this journey pretty well, some of them walked 25 miles without tasting a mouthful of anything and a scanty supper at that."[42] The hot weather made "some of the brethren sick and obliged [them] to ride in the baggage wagons." While the Battalion remained "in good spirits" they ran out of flour at one point and "had parched corn for supper."[43] The men fashioned rudimentary skewers from sticks, wrapped raw dough around the sticks, and held them over the fire. A number of them resorted to appropriating all kinds of crops from the fields they passed through. "Vegetables were a treat to persons living principally on bread and bacon," explained Henry Sanderson. Chickens, beehives, pigs, and ears of corn grown by local farmers suffered the same fate, leaving one farmer "a very mad man using very bad language."[44]

The only casualty on this preliminary leg of the journey occurred on the second day of the march. Samuel Boley of Company B had been sick in Council Bluffs even before he enlisted. Despite efforts to prevent him from joining the Battalion march to Fort Leavenworth, Boley stubbornly insisted on going; he died on the evening of July 22.[45] The following day his corpse was "wrapped in his blanket and buried in a rough lumber coffin, which was the best we could get."[46]

The allegiance and bond of the men toward Lieutenant Colonel Allen strengthened as they traveled toward Fort Leavenworth. He possessed an endearing quality that drew the Battalion to him unlike any of his successors, despite the Mormon distrust of the government he represented. An event mentioned by numerous diarists solidified Allen's place in the hearts and minds of his soldiers.

A hired man from Missouri arrived in camp with much-needed flour; when he learned that the Battalion was comprised of Mormons, he refused to deliver the flour. Upon learning of the ordeal, Allen was insulted and "gave him a severe reprimand and ordered the flour into camp forthwith, it accordingly came."[47] The camp resonated with shouts of "God bless the Colonel!"

The difficulty in this first leg of the trek was not the steepness of the terrain or the threat of combat, but rather the sweltering temperatures, a shortage of food, and the fresh heartache of deserting loved ones in uncertain circumstances to fend for themselves and rely on the assistance of fellow Saints. The only real danger encountered on the trail from Council Bluffs to Fort Leavenworth occurred near Bloomington on the evening of July 30, when a violent storm took out trees and killed an ox. Henry Standage recorded:

> Almost 9 o'clock P.M. the wind commenced blowing very hard and continued to blow until the trees fell in all directions around the camp; the brethren were all aroused from sleep and out of their wigwams, which were built of bushes, looking for those in the camp to fall every minute, there was about 80 fires kindled for the cooking of supper, which had died away but enlivened up again by the wind blowing so hard, which together with the lightning which was very vivid, had a curious appearance and was alarming considering the crashing of timber, howling of the wind &c. but not one tree fell in camp—which proved to us that God was with us, the cattle were in an old field where there was some deadened trees, and one ox was killed.[48]

Before entering Fort Leavenworth, the men paused at a small creek to wash their clothes. All five companies arrived on August 1 in the early afternoon, joining six additional companies comprised of Missouri volunteers. The men were grateful to have Lieutenant Colonel Allen issue tents after traveling twelve days and "180 miles without tents camping out and lying on the ground."[49] The following day a messenger reported to Church leaders that the Battalion was well and in good spirits and "doing honor to the cause."[50]

About the same time that Captain Allen and his battalion of Mormons arrived at Fort Leavenworth, Brigham Young and Church leaders abandoned their hopes of reaching the Rockies in 1846 and made plans to winter on the west side of the Missouri River. The loss of nearly five hundred men to the Mexican War was the last of a number of factors that halted the westward migration of the Church and delayed the first pioneer company from reaching the Salt Lake Valley until July 1847. This preliminary leg of the march to the Pacific was quite uneventful and the terrain was much easier than what the Battalion would later encounter. Boley's death was unrelated to the physical demands of the trek, and trials associated with heat and lack of food would pale in comparison to what the group would experience on the Cimarron cutoff and beyond. For the Battalion soldiers, the journey had just begun, and the arduous road they would soon follow to Santa Fe was fraught with changes in leadership, extreme conditions, and physical exertion that stretched the men to their limits, even bringing some to the grave.

Endnotes

1 "A Circular of the High Council," *Times and Seasons* 6, no. 21 (January 15, 1846), 1096.

2 Jesse C. Little's report as quoted in B. H. Roberts, *A Comprehensive History of the Church of Jesus Christ of Latter-day Saints*, 6 vols. (Salt Lake City: Deseret News Press, 1930), 3:67–68.

3 See Matthew J. Grow, *"Liberty to the Downtrodden": Thomas L. Kane, Romantic Reformer* (New Haven, CT: Yale University Press, 2009), 47–53.

4 Kendall was postmaster general for Andrew Jackson and Martin Van Buren. He served as an unofficial adviser to Polk during his presidency.

5 For recent works on the Mexican War, see John S. D. Eisenhower, *So Far from God: The U.S. War with Mexico, 1846–1848* (New York: Random House, 1989); Timothy J. Henderson, *A Glorious Defeat: Mexico and Its War with the United States* (New York: Hill & Wang, 2007); and Richard Bruce Winders, *Mr. Polk's Army: The American Military Experience in the Mexican American War* (College Station, TX: Texas A&M University Press, 1997). The estimate of the present-day costs of the war is found in Stephen Daggett, "Costs of Major U.S. Wars," Congressional Research Service Report for Congress, 29 June 2010, accessed 12 December 2011, http://www.fas.org/sgp/crs/natsec/RS22926.pdf.

6 Jesse C. Little to President James K. Polk, 1 June 1846, as quoted in Bigler and Bagley, eds., *Army of Israel*, 32–35.

7 The Oregon question was resolved with the signing of the Oregon Treaty by Britain and the United States on 15 June 1846 in Washington, DC.

8 Milo Milton Quaife, ed., *Diary of James K. Polk during His Presidency, 1845 to 1848*, 4 vols. (Chicago: A. C. McClurg & Co., 1910), 1:443–450.

9 Ibid., 1:446.

10 Stephen Watts Kearny to James Allen, 19 June 1846, as quoted in Tyler, *A Concise History of the Mormon Battalion*, 113–114.

11 Wilford Woodruff, Journal, 26 June 1846, in Kenney, ed., *Wilford Woodruff's Journal*, 3:55

12 Hosea Stout, *On the Mormon Frontier: the Diary of Hosea Stout, 1844–1861*, edited by Juanita Brooks, 2 vols. (Salt Lake City: University of Utah Press, 1982), 1:172.

13 "Circular to the Mormons," quoted in Tyler, *A Concise History of the Mormon Battalion*, 114–115.

14 William Clayton, Journal, 27 June 1846, Church History Library.

15 Albert Smith, Reminiscences and Journal, Typescript, 22, Church History Library.

16 Fleek, *History May Be Searched in Vain*, 27–28.

17 Manuscript History of the Mormon Battalion, 20 July 1846, Church History Library.

18 Journal History of The Church of Jesus Christ of Latter-day Saints, 1 July 1846, Church History Library.

19 Watson, ed., *Manuscript History of Brigham Young*, 222.

20 Henry W. Bigler, Memoir, 40, Church History Library.

21 Hyde wrote retrospectively, since Brigham Young did not become president of the Church until December 1847. William Hyde, 16 July 1846, as cited in Manuscript History of the Mormon Battalion; William Hyde, *The Private Journal of William Hyde*, 18.

22 Samuel H. Rogers, Reminiscences and Diary, 5 July 1846, Church History Library.

23 Grow, *Liberty to the Downtrodden*, 49.

24 Woodruff, Journal, 11 July 1846, in Kenney, ed., *Wilford Woodruff's Journal*, 3:58.

25 Journal History, 16 July 1846, Church History Library; Richard E. Bennett, *Mormons at the Missouri: Winter Quarters, 1846–1852* (Norman, OK: University of Oklahoma Press, 2004), 73.

26 Tyler, *A Concise History of the Mormon Battalion*, 156–157.

27 Henry W. Bigler, Memoir, 40, Church History Library.

28 Woodruff, Journal, 16 July 1846, in Kenney, ed., *Wilford Woodruff's*, 3:60.

29 William Hyde, 18 July 1846, in *The Private Journal of William Hyde*, 19.

30 Journal History, 18 July 1846, Church History Library.

31 Manuscript History of the Mormon Battalion, 18 July 1846, Church History Library.

32 Kane's account in Tyler, *A Concise History of the Mormon Battalion*, 81.

33 Henry W. Bigler, Memoir, 40–41, Church History Library.

34 Samuel Gould in Company C was the oldest of the Battalion recruits at sixty-seven, while Alfred Higgins was only fourteen and served under Captain Nelson Higgins, his father, in Company D.

35 James Allen, Return for 31 July 1846, Mexican War

Service Records, 1845–1848, Record Group 94, National Archives as quoted in Fleek, *History May Be Searched in Vain*, 145; see also Ricketts, *The Mormon Battalion: U.S. Army of the West*, 20–28.

36 Zadok Knapp Judd, Autobiography, 21, Church History Library.

37 James S. Brown, quoted in Tyler, *A Concise History of the Mormon Battalion*, 357.

38 George Washington Taggart to Fanny Parks Taggart, 8 July 1846, Church History Library.

39 William Hyde, 17 July 1846, in *The Private Journal of William Hyde*, 18–19.

40 Henry Standage, Journal, 20 July 1846, in Frank Alfred Golder, ed., *The March of the Mormon Battalion from Council Bluffs to California: Taken from the Journal of Henry Standage* (New York: The Century Co., 1928), 139.

41 George P. Dykes to Diantha, Alcina, and Cynthia Dykes, 29 July 1846, Mormon Battalion correspondence collection, Church History Library.

42 John Steele, Journal, 24 July 1846, Church History Library.

43 Standage, Journal, 25 July 1846, in Golder, ed., *The March of the Mormon Battalion*, 139–140.

44 Henry W. Sanderson, Autobiography, typescript, 37, Church History Library.

45 Standage, Journal, 22 July 1846, in Golder, ed., *The March of the Mormon Battalion*, 139.

46 Tyler, *A Concise History of the Mormon Battalion*, 131; Standage, 23 July 1846.

47 Standage, Journal, 27 July 1846, in Golder, ed., *The March of the Mormon Battalion*, 140.

48 Ibid., 30 July 1846, in Golder, ed., *The March of the Mormon Battalion*, 141.

49 Ibid., 1 August 1846, in Golder, ed., *The March of the Mormon Battalion*, 141–142.

50 Woodruff, Journal, 2 August 1846, in Kenney, ed., *Wilford Woodruff's Journal*, 3:64.

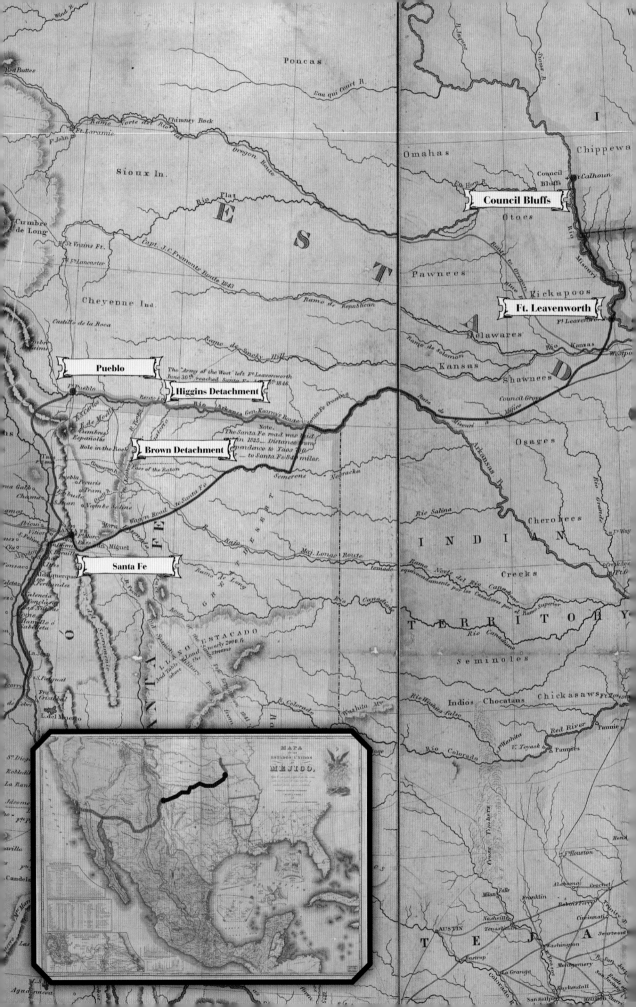

Chapter Three

FORT LEAVENWORTH TO SANTA FE

"A hevy load for A Mule"

A rriving at Fort Leavenworth on August 1, the new soldiers received their first taste of military life. During the almost two-week stay, their enlistment in a wartime army became a sobering reality. After being issued muskets and accoutrements, Private Albert Smith wryly noted that it would be "A hevy load for A Mule."[1] Within the first few days of the march toward Santa Fe, with the August sun beating down and each man carrying as much as forty-five pounds of equipment, Smith probably reflected more than once about being loaded down like a pack mule.[2]

At Fort Leavenworth, Battalion members received everything necessary to distinguish them as soldiers with one exception—they received no uniforms. Even if the men had wanted uniforms, probably none were available because General Stephen W. Kearny's units, which left weeks before the Mormon Battalion arrived at Fort Leavenworth, likely took the fort's supply of uniforms for themselves.[3]

Each man was allotted forty-five dollars as a clothing allowance. A portion of the $21,000 that the Battalion collectively received for

The Mormon Battalion reached Fort Leavenworth on August 1, 1846, under the leadership of Captain James Allen. Much of the money allocated to the men by the U.S. Army at the fort as a clothing allowance was donated to the Church and sent back to Council Bluffs. (Courtesy of Wisconsin State Historical Society, WHS-23983.)

John Steele (1821–1903) was a member of Company D and one of many that chronicled their experiences in the Mormon Battalion. (Courtesy of Church History Library.)

Daniel Tyler (1816–1906) was a sergeant in Company C and published an important book titled *A Concise History of the Mormon Battalion in the Mexican War, 1846–1847* in 1881. (Courtesy of International Society Daughters of Utah Pioneers, Salt Lake City.)

clothing, as well as a percentage of the pay received during their service—"apparently well in excess of $50,000"—was donated by the soldiers to the Church. These funds, donated at a time when the Church was desperately short of resources, proved to be a great blessing.[4] Parley P. Pratt, Orson Hyde, John Taylor, and Jesse C. Little reached Fort Leavenworth on August 5 and received a little more than $5,000 in clothing allowance funds donated by Battalion members for the Church.[5] Pratt delivered the funds on his return to Council Bluffs. Battalion members also used some of the clothing allowance for items they needed or retained the funds for their families. John Steele, for example, "sent $10 to the [Council] Bluffs—$6.00 to Louis Zebriskie and $4.00 to the poor. $10.00 I also lent to the Captain of our Company, Nelson Higgans, and some to help the brethren going to the Bluffs."[6]

In addition, the soldiers occupied their time purchasing personal items from local traders, writing letters to family, receiving instruction on basic drills, and even baptizing one man, John Allen, who joined the Mormon Battalion as a member of Company E. In addition to those Battalion soldiers who became ill during the march from Council Bluffs to Fort Leavenworth, several more became sick during their sojourn at the fort.

Twelve days after arrival at the fort, Mormon Battalion companies A, B, and E began the march to Santa Fe. Companies C and D, which had "remained behind to rig themselves out a little better for the journey," caught up with the first three companies on August 19.[7] The stifling weather continued to afflict the men. John Steele noted, "The weather is very hot, amounting almost to suffocation."[8] They were also minus their commander, as James Allen became so ill at Fort Leavenworth that he could no longer lead the Battalion; he remained at the fort. For the only time during their entire one-year enlistment, the soldiers of the Mormon Battalion were under the interim command of one of their own officers, Captain Jefferson Hunt.[9]

On August 26, near Council Grove—a major staging area for freight caravans on the Santa Fe Trail—Samuel Gully brought news from Fort Leavenworth that Allen had died. Sergeant Reddick N. Allred (whose name is sometimes spelled Redick in historical accounts) noted, "At the sound of the Drums muffled we were called to pay our respects to Lieut. Col. Allen our late commander who died at Fort Leavenworth after our march from that place . . ."[10] Just two days later, on August 28, Daniel Tyler described the death of a couple who had been traveling with the Battalion:

an aged English lady by the name of Jane Bosco,
who was traveling in company with Captain Hunt,

Fort Leavenworth
Aug.t 23d 1846

President Brigham Young
    Sir

        It is with the deepest regret
that I have to inform you of the death of Lt
Col. James Allen, late commander of the Mormon
Battallion. The command left this post last
week and is now encamped about 40 Miles from
here. The particulars of the lamented & universal
favorite Col. Allen will be communicated to you by
Lt (james) oled the bearer of this note. If it is the wish
of your people that I should take charge of the
Battallion, and conduct it to Gen.l Kearny, I will
do it with pleasure & feel proud of the command.
I have in my possession most, if not all the papers
that relate to the movements of this Battallion, & will
use my best endeavors to see all orders & promises heretofore
given, carried into execution.

                    I am Sir
                Very Respectfully
                    Your Ob.t Serv.t
                    A. J. Smith
                    1st Dragoons.

died, and her husband—not a soldier—died before
daylight the next morning. Thus they gained an oft-
repeated wish that neither should be left to mourn
the loss of the other. They were very highly respected.
They were buried in one grave, and a dry substantial
stone wall was built around and over the tomb . . .
The covering was of good but unpolished flat rock.[11]

This letter was written by Andrew Jackson Smith to inform Brigham Young of Captain James Allen's death on August 23, 1846, at Fort Leavenworth. (Courtesy of Church History Library.)

Andrew Jackson Smith (1815–1897) served as the commander of the Battalion from late August until mid-October, following the death of James Allen. This image was taken during the Civil War. (Courtesy of the Library of Congress.)

Jefferson Hunt (1804–1879) was the captain of Company A in the Mormon Battalion. In the years following his July 1847 discharge from the U.S. Army, Hunt helped settle San Bernardino, served in the California State Assembly, and represented Weber County in the Utah Territorial Legislature. (Courtesy of Church History Library.)

On August 30, the day following the burial, U.S. Army Lieutenant Andrew Jackson Smith and U. S. Army surgeon George B. Sanderson, along with their staffs, arrived at the Battalion's camp at Council Grove. Smith fully expected to take command of the Battalion, since he had the verbal approval of Fort Leavenworth's commanding officer, Lieutenant Colonel Clifton Wharton.[12] Their arrival was a pivotal moment for the Mormon Battalion, because decisions about whether leadership should be military or ecclesiastical created tensions among the ranks that simmered throughout the rest of the march.

Captain Jefferson Hunt and most other company officers decided that Smith should assume command of the Battalion in light of his experience, training, and knowledge of military procedure. In addition, because the Mormon Battalion officers had no signed commissions from President Polk or any other recognized government authority, they really had no legitimate right to command, a fact Hunt expressed in a letter to Brigham Young.[13] Many of the soldiers resented the change in command, particularly because Hunt and the other officers had not sought their opinion. Within a month, the Mormon Battalion had experienced three changes of command—Lieutenant Colonel James Allen, Captain Jefferson Hunt, and now Lieutenant Andrew Jackson Smith. When they finally reached Santa Fe, there would be one last change of command—Colonel Philip St. George Cooke would lead them to the Pacific coast.

Even thornier than the question of command, the medical orders of the military doctor—George B. Sanderson, who accompanied Smith—became a source of bitterness to many of the soldiers. As a Missourian, Sanderson was already viewed with suspicion by many Mormon Battalion members who had endured extreme persecution the previous decade while living in Missouri. In addition, Sanderson insisted throughout the march that when ill, Battalion soldiers submit to a regimen of medicines he prescribed. Most soldiers, however, were intent on following a policy suggested in a letter from Brigham Young, in which he advised, "If you are sick, live by faith, and let the surgeon's medicine alone if you want to live, using only such herbs and mild food as are at your disposal. If you give heed to this counsel, you will prosper; but if not, we cannot be responsible for the consequences."[14]

Given the world view held by Tyler and some of the others in the Battalion, Sanderson's motives were always questioned. However, historian Sherman Fleek, in analyzing mid-nineteenth-century U. S. military medical standards, determined that Sanderson was following the medical practices of the day and found that Sanderson's own journal entries provided a different perspective on the doctor than the views of some in the Battalion: "George Sanderson's journal contradicts the impression that many have held for years . . . Throughout his entire journal, there is no criticism of his Mormon charges,

August 24th 1846 Left Fort Leavenworth Monday morning in company with Lt Smith 1st Dragoons we travelled on to the Stranger river distance about 24 or 25 miles from the Fort we spent our time in talking about those we had left behind us. the country we passed over was beautifully undulating, and well watered; at this River we parted, Mr Smith to wait the arrival of his waggon, I to overtake mine which started the day previous to me. I succeeded in overtaking in about two miles from the Stranger. The responsibility of pitching Tents preparing for Supper &c produced rather a singular feeling. I found upon examination I had no coffee pot the key of my mess chest lost or mislaid. I had to content myself with such a supper as I could get, it consisted of hard bread broiled bacon & water, not a bad neither for a Soldier, went to bed early and slept well. Augst 25th got up at daylight found my cooks busy preparing breakfast, which consisted of Irish potatoes, broiled bacon, and something they called coffee boiled in a large camp kettle. I relished it very well my appetite being good. we left camp about seven oclock and proceeded on to the Kansas river and there waited the arrival of Lt Smith, who came up in about two hours, we crossed the River and arrived at Hurricane point about six oclock and encamped. this place accrues its name from the Mormon Battalion being overtaken here by a very severe hurricane. I have just bid farewell to all appearances of Civilization having passed the last cultivated spot I expect to see in the U.S. untill I return. our cook is preparing supper and I anticipate rather a better one than I had last night; the country passed over to day is Prairie occasionally interspersed with timber. one thing I forgot to note Lt Smiths team failing to pull up a hill myself Smith and the force we could muster was required to get the waggon up the hill, we finally succeeded. Smith made a very important discovery after we arrived in camp and that was a bottle of very fine old whisky as a matter of course it was attended to. we travelled to day about 18 miles had a good supper smoked a Segar and went to bed Augst 26th

August 1846 entries from Dr. George B. Sanderson's diary. Sanderson (1800–1861) was appointed as assistant surgeon to the Mormon Battalion and was the source of contention among many of the soldiers due to his Missouri roots and Brigham Young's advice to "let the surgeon's medicine alone." (Courtesy of Special Collections, J. Willard Marriott Library, University of Utah.)

no aspersions against any single man or soldier, no bias or prejudice against the Latter-day Saints and their religious faith."[15]

Sanderson's Missouri roots and his demand for strict obedience to military orders, often coupled with an apparent shortage of interpersonal skills, contributed to the divisive issue of medical treatment. Even if these issues could have been resolved, military medical practice stood in stark contrast with the insistence by some in the Battalion of a literal adherence to Brigham Young's counsel to "let the surgeon's medicine alone."[16] The two seemingly irreconcilable positions proved to be a prescription for conflict in the ensuing months of the march.

For those in the Battalion, the rigors of the march always made health a concern. The numbers who became ill began to swell after September 10, when the Battalion was ordered to take the shorter Cimarron Cutoff rather than continue to Bent's Fort before turning south to Santa Fe. Henry Standage noted, "This morning while we were in camp an express came from Santa Fe on their way to Fort Leavenworth, who gave us news of the surrender of that place. The Gen. marching in without the firing of a gun and bringing us advice from the Gen. to take the Semiron trail, leaving Bent's Fort to our left."[17] Because it saved time, the Cimarron Cutoff was more commonly traveled in the 1840s than the route through Bent's Fort. The downside to the Cimarron was the lack of reliable water sources and feed. Those traveling the Cimarron Cutoff had to ensure there were sufficient provisions before attempting it.

Following the cutoff, the Battalion reached the Arkansas River on September 15, where they met Colonel Sterling Price and the five hundred cavalrymen of the Missouri Mounted Volunteers under his command. The encounter was probably tense, since Price was remembered by many of the soldiers as a Missouri mobber who drove the Mormons from Missouri. Writing retrospectively, Henry Bigler recounted a story related to him by fellow Battalion member Lisborn Lamb:

Colonel Sterling Price (1809–1867), pictured in the center, was commander of the Second Regiment of the Missouri Volunteers and numbered among the mobs that drove the Mormons out of Missouri in the 1830s. This image was taken during his service in the Civil War. (Courtesy of National Archives.)

When the battalion over<took> Colonel Sterling Price at the crossing of the Arkansas[,] Colonel Smith being short of provisions Sent his quarter master to ask Price to Share provision with him. Price Said he did not haul provisions for the mormons. this intelligence raised Col Smiths ire and he sent word back to Price that if he did not let the provisions come that he would let loose the mormons and come down on him with his artillery when this on the part of Colonel Smith produced the desired effect. Here I will say that Colonel Price was in command of a company of mob militia at Far West and Sanctioned the Shooting of joseph the Prophet and others on the public Square in 38 and this Col Smith may have known and thought that the "mormons" had but little use for him, hence the threat to come down on him by letting loose the mormons etc.[18]

The potential for trouble with Price and his troops would surface again later in Santa Fe.

Although thirst was temporarily allayed for Price's troops and the Battalion at the Arkansas River, illness among Battalion soldiers continued unabated. Alva Phelps, who had not completely recovered from illness contracted at Fort Leavenworth, died and was buried on September 17 at their camp where the Cimarron Cutoff crossed the Arkansas River.[19] Back at Council Bluffs, Alva's wife Margaret was dealing with her own illness, among other difficulties. In 1878 she retrospectively wrote of this difficult time in a letter to former Battalion member Daniel Tyler:

> We were traveling when the call came for him to leave us . . . I was very ill at the time, my children all small, my babe also extremely sick; but the call was pressing . . . He left in the morning. I watched him from my wagon-bed till his loved form was lost in the distance; it was my last sight of him.
>
> Two months from the day of his enlistment, the sad news of my bereavement arrived. This blow entirely prostrated me. But I had just embarked on my sea of troubles; winter found me bed-ridden, destitute, in a wretched hovel which was built upon a hillside; the season was one of constant rain; the situation of the hovel and its openness, gave free access to piercing winds and water flowed over the dirt floor, converting it into mud two or three inches deep; no wood but what my little ones picked up around the fences, so green it filled the room with smoke; the rain dropping and wetting the bed which I was powerless to leave.[20]

Some soldiers, including Tyler, became convinced that Sanderson poisoned Phelps and that the doctor's sole objective was to poison as many in the Mormon Battalion as possible. After Phelps died, Tyler wrote:

He begged Dr. Sanderson not to give him any strong medicine, as he needed only a little rest and then would return to duty; but the Doctor prepared his dose and ordered him to take it, which he declined doing, whereupon the Doctor, with some horrid oaths, forced it down him with the old rusty spoon. A few hours later he died, and the general feeling was that the Doctor had killed him. Many boldly expressed the opinion that it was a case of premeditated murder. When we consider the many murderous threats previously made, this conclusion is by no means far–fetched.[21]

Whether Phelps would have survived if the Battalion had continued to Bent's Fort is uncertain. Although Smith did follow orders to travel the Cimarron Cutoff, on September 15 he also ordered some in the Battalion to travel along the Arkansas River to Bent's Fort on detached service under the command of Captain Nelson Higgins.

Although Captain Allen had intended the Mormon Battalion to follow the Santa Fe Trail to Bent's Fort, only the Higgins detachment did so while the rest of the Battalion followed the shorter Cimarron Cutoff. The Higgins detachment did not stop at Bent's Fort, but continued on to Pueblo in present-day Colorado. They opted to push on to Pueblo instead of wintering at Bent's Fort after learning that some Latter-day Saints from Mississippi were already at Pueblo, intending to travel north in the spring and

Sketch of buffalo by Frederick Piercy published in *Route from Liverpool to Great Salt Lake Valley*, 1855. (Courtesy of Church History Library.)

meet up with the main body of Saints headed west. A few of the men among the "Mississippi Saints" had come west without their families and decided to return to Mississippi and escort them back to Pueblo. On their return to Mississippi they encountered the Mormon Battalion on September 11. It was from this encounter that the Battalion members learned about the Pueblo settlement.[22]

The Higgins "detachment" was the first of three detachments from the Battalion; Colonel Philip St. George Cooke ordered the other two, one in mid-October and the last during the second week of November. These three detachments have loosely been described as "sick detachments." That descriptive phrase is not entirely accurate as evidenced by the fact that Alva Phelps, obviously ill, was not included in the Higgins detachment that left the Battalion in mid-September. All three detachments eventually arrived in Pueblo, where they remained during the winter of 1846–1847.

Still, there was no question that traveling the Cimarron Cutoff instead of continuing to Bent's Fort proved more difficult because, as Daniel Tyler recorded, "the most of the provisions etc., and two pieces of artillery, were in advance of us toward the former place, where we understood our lamented Colonel, James Allen, designed us to winter, in case we were too late to cross the mountains that fall."[23] September 17—the day Phelps died—Lieutenant James Pace of Company E, along with John D. Lee and Howard Egan, caught up with the Battalion, intending to take some of the Battalion payroll back to Church leaders in Council Bluffs. They traveled with the unit along the Cimarron Cutoff to Santa Fe. In his short stay with the Battalion, Lee sought to negate Smith's right to command and complained bitterly about many of his orders to the soldiers—all to no avail. After receiving some of the Battalion payroll in Santa Fe, Lee and Egan returned to Council Bluffs.

While the Cimarron Cutoff was shorter, continuing heat, the shortage of provisions, and the lack of reliable water sources caused severe suffering among the soldiers. Graphic descriptions from their diaries of the water quality attest to what thirst can do. Tyler recalled:

> We passed one lone pond full of insects of all sizes and shapes. Out of this pond we drove several thousand Buffalo. . . . The water . . . was discolored and had a most disgusting appearance. The animals, doubtless, rendered it more noisome than it otherwise would have been by gathering in it to defend themselves from the flies. . . . No luxury was ever more thankfully received. The few whose canteens and flagons were not exhausted, of course did not use it, but, bad as it was, it was very welcome to the most of us."[24]

Henry Bigler noted its effect on some soldiers:

> We marched twenty-five miles and encamped
> without water for our animals and a very scanty
> supply for the men. That day was very warm; teams
> gave out and men, too, for want of water. The men
> who had given out had to be brought to camp
> in wagons. After we had marched about twenty
> miles, we came to a small dirty, muddy pond of
> water tramped up by the buffalo. The water was
> well mixed with their green manure. . . . The men
> drank without complaining, but gracious how sick
> it made some of them."[25]

Not everything about the march was drudgery and suffering.
On September 29, John Steele wrote:

> Started and came 6 miles along the Rabbit
> Ears Mountains. I went ahunting in company with
> Brother Thomas W. Treat. Went about five miles
> off the road. Discovered 24 antelope. Fired and
> missed. . . .[26]

However, there was little time for diversions. While on the
Cimarron Cutoff, Lieutenant Smith learned that General Stephen
Watts Kearny planned to discharge the Mormon Battalion if it did
not reach Santa Fe by October 10. Anxious to retain his command,
Smith was determined to reach Santa Fe by that date. John Steele
noted the effect of the division on the men:

> Sat. [October] 3rd. Came seven miles and
> camped where there was a project got up by Lieu-
> tenant Smith, who took the command of us at the
> Council Grove, after the death of Lt. Colonel Al-
> len, that the one-half of our company was to go
> ahead and leave the rest to follow when and how
> they could, so this evening 50 men from each
> company was selected and left us and went ahead.
> We were all very vexed to part, but those who are
> bound must obey.[27]

The Battalion soldiers were dissatisfied with the division because Brigham Young had been assured by Captain James Allen
in July that the Battalion would remain together as a unit; Smith
had already sent one "sick" detachment to winter on the Arkansas River at Pueblo under the command of Captain Higgins. On

October 8, a day before reaching Santa Fe, an express passed bearing news, undoubtedly disheartening to Smith, that the "General had appointed Captain Cooke, Company K, 1st Dragoons, to the command of the Battalion." Although Smith no longer had reason to continue the forced march, the Battalion still marched fifteen miles that day.[28] Perhaps he still held a glimmer of hope that he would be given a command. One fact was certain: unless he met the October 10 deadline, the Battalion would be discharged and there would be no soldiers for him to lead should an opportunity to command arise.

As the Battalion approached Santa Fe, some soldiers noted the changes in the architecture of the settlements they passed. On October 7, William Coray wrote, "Marched 18 miles, passed the town of San Magual [Miguel], the English of it is St. Michiel [Michael] which contains a cathedral church and about 150 houses which were built of brick about four times as large as United States bricks."[29] Unfamiliar with Spanish architectural styles, William Coray also noted the adobe appearance of Santa Fe, describing it as "a large brick yard. On entering the city their houses bear the resemblance of kilns of unburnt brick."[30] David Pettigrew described Santa Fe as "an old town; the Spanish houses are of curious workmanship, flat tops covered with cement that will not leak." He also included an odd observation about the residents, declaring, "They are catholics and appear to be of the jewish race."[31]

John Steele recorded that he and the balance of the Battalion "came 14 miles through the mountains and at last came to the far famed city of Santa Fe about 5 p.m. The American Flag floats high in the air. The city extends 5 miles long and looks like a very large brick yard. They have to water their grounds from rivers that run

An 1848 lithograph of Santa Fe by Curtis B. Graham. When the Mormon Battalion arrived in Santa Fe in October 1846, many of the soldiers were captivated by the architecture of the bustling town. (Courtesy of Beinecke Rare Book and Manuscript Library, Yale University.)

through their city. Their houses are one story high, flat roofed and very comfortable inside."[32]

On October 9, a day before Kearny's deadline, the first portion of the Mormon Battalion marched into town in military order and encamped on the east of three divisions stationed there. The balance of the companies arrived in Santa Fe on October 11 and 12. As the first Mormon Battalion soldiers arrived, General Alexander Doniphan's Missouri troops honored them by firing a salute "of one hundred guns . . . from the roofs of houses" and he "received them with friendship. Wood, feed and provisions were hauled to their quarters immediately."[33] In the 1830s during the Latter-day Saint troubles in Missouri, Doniphan had won the enduring affection and gratitude of the Mormons for his refusal to carry out an order to execute Joseph Smith and several other Mormons who were prisoners of the Missouri militia. Now, almost a decade later, Doniphan's salute to the Mormon Battalion as it entered Santa Fe affirmed the depth of that friendship.

Doniphan afforded no such salute to Colonel Sterling Price and his cavalry. Tyler recorded that, "When Colonel Sterling price with his cavalry command which left Fort Leavenworth two or three days ahead of us, arrived at Santa Fe, he was received without any public demonstration, and when he learned of the salute which had been fired in honor of the 'Mormons,' he was greatly chagrinned and enraged."[34]

It appeared that the Mormons faced more trouble from Price and his Missouri units than from the Mexicans. Weeks before their arrival, Kearny had taken the New Mexico province without any armed conflict. Private Henry Standage described the capitulation of Santa Fe as providential: "The Mexicans had 6,000 at this place and Gen. Kearney but 1,800, and yet the Mexicans fled from the pass and Kearney with his army of 1,800 marched through into Santa Fe, whose population was about 6,000; not a gun was fired. Surely the Lord is on our side and is opening the way before us, so that we may march into the Upper California without the shedding of blood. All praise be ascribed to God and his Son."[35]

In preparing to march, Colonel Cooke now assumed leadership over the Mormon companies and decided that the Battalion was "enlisted too much by families; some were too old, some feeble, and some too young."[36] He detached a number of women, children, and sick Battalion members under the command of Captain James

Brown to backtrack and winter with the Higgins detachment, by now at Pueblo. Henry Bigler was despondent about the decision, as "in that detachment I had a dear sister and brother in law John W. Hess. I felt lonesome after they left, for I missed their company very much. they left on the 18th."[37]

The following day at noon, Cooke and the balance of the Mormon Battalion began the march from Santa Fe to the Pacific. The just-completed leg of the journey, from Fort Leavenworth to Santa Fe, had taken two months. During that time the soldiers marched more than seven hundred difficult miles. Loaded down with their military equipment, they experienced fatigue and exhaustion, constant thirst from the blistering heat of the late summer sun, and frequent hunger from the lack of provisions. They also experienced the death of some companions, the detachment of others to a winter camp at Pueblo, three changes in command, and, for many, an accelerated march to Santa Fe ordered by Smith to meet a seemingly impractical arrival deadline imposed upon them by General Kearny.

In these months of travel toward Santa Fe, the mostly young men who composed the Mormon Battalion were also exposed to a world they knew nothing about. They learned what it meant to be a soldier, saw remarkable landscapes, and encountered new cultures. They engaged in self-assessment while internalizing the new, difficult, or unfamiliar experiences through which they passed. Individually, they began to understand that they could endure more, accomplish more, and, most importantly, become more than they ever thought possible. The march to Santa Fe began to permanently alter and broaden their worldview. This transformative process would continue throughout their wartime service and in the end it created a great reservoir of mature, experienced men whose wisdom and service would be a blessing to the Church and its members for decades.

Endnotes

1   Albert Smith, Reminiscences and Journal, 5 August 1846, Church History Library.

2   For a description of equipment US infantrymen were issued and expected to carry, see Val John Halford, *Mormon Battalion: Military Arms, Equipment, and Training* (printed by author, 2004).

3   Fleek, *History May Be Searched in Vain*, 154–155.

4   Leonard J. Arrington, *Great Basin Kingdom: An Economic History of the Latter-day Saints, 1830–1900* (Cambridge, MA: Harvard University Press, 1958; reprint from Urbana, IL: University of Illinois, 2005), 20, 55; see also John F. G. Yurtinus, "A Ram in the Thicket: The Mormon Battalion in the Mexican War" (PhD dissertation, Brigham Young University, 1976), 639; Ricketts, *The Mormon Battalion: U.S. Army of the West*, 70; Fleek, *History May Be Searched in Vain*, 238.

5   Manuscript History of the Mormon Battalion, 5 August 1846, Church History Library.

6   John Steele, Diary, 7 August 1846, typescript, Church History Library.

7   William Coray, Journal, 13 August 1846, quoted in Ricketts, *The Mormon Battalion: U.S. Army of the West*, 41.

8   Steele, Diary, 15 August 1846, typescript, Church History Library.

9   Tyler, *A Concise History of the Mormon Battalion*, 137–138.

10 Robert S. Bliss, Diary, typescript, 29 September 1846, Church History Library.

11 Tyler, *A Concise History of the Mormon Battalion*, 142.

12 Smith's temporary assumption of command was legitimate. For an insightful analysis, see Fleek, *History May Be Searched in Vain*, 171–175.

13 Jefferson Hunt to Brigham Young, 17 October 1846, Brigham Young Office Files, Church History Library.

14 Brigham Young to Jefferson Hunt, 19 August 1846, quoted in Tyler, *A Concise History of the Mormon Battalion*, 146.

15 Fleek, *History May Be Searched in Vain*, 195–196.

16 Ibid., 193.

17 Henry Standage, 10 September 1846, in Golder, ed., *The March of the Mormon Battalion*, 161.

18 Henry W. Bigler, Memoir, 46–47, Church History Library.

19 Ibid.

20 Phelps to Tyler, 30 April 1878, quoted in Tyler, *A Concise History of the Mormon Battalion*, 129. See also Bennett, *Mormons at the Missouri*, 79–80.

21 Tyler, *A Concise History of the Mormon Battalion*, 158.

22 John Z. Brown, "Pioneer Journeys from Nauvoo, Illinois to Pueblo, Colorado in 1846, and over the Plains in 1847: Extracts from the Private Journal of the Late Pioneer John Brown, who for a Period of Twenty-Nine Years was Bishop of Pleasant Grove," *Improvement Era* (July 1910), 803–810. For a detailed account of the sick detachments in Pueblo, see Yurtinus, "A Ram in the Thicket: The Mormon Battalion in the Mexican War."

23 Daniel Tyler, 10 September 1846, quoted in Manuscript History of the Mormon Battalion; Tyler, *A Concise History of the Mormon Battalion*, 148–149.

24 Tyler, *A Concise History of the Mormon Battalion*, 159.

25 Erwin G. Gudde, *Bigler's Chronicle of the West: The Conquest of California, Discovery of Gold, and Mormon Settlement as Reflected in Henry William Bigler's Diaries* (Berkeley, CA: University of California Press, 1962), 26.

26 Steele, Diary, 29 September 1846, typescript, Church History Library.

27 Ibid., 3 October 1846.

28 Manuscript History of the Mormon Battalion, 8 October 1846, Church History Library.

29 Ibid., 7 October 1846.

30 William Coray, 9 October 1846, quoted in Manuscript History of the Mormon Battalion, Church History Library.

31 David Pettigrew, Journal, 10 October 1846, David Pettigrew collection, 1836–1883; 1926–1930, Church History Library.

32 Steele, Diary, 12 October 1846, Church History Library.

33 Tyler, *A Concise History of the Mormon Battalion*, 164; Manuscript History of the Mormon Battalion, 9 October 1846, Church History Library.

34 Tyler, *A Concise History of the Mormon Battalion*, 164.

35 Standage, 9 October 1846, in Golder, ed., *The March of the Mormon Battalion*, 170–171.

36   Phillip St. George Cooke, *The Conquest of New Mexico and California: An Historical and Personal Narrative* (New York: G. P. Putnam's Sons, 1878), 91.

37   Henry W. Bigler, Memoir, 47, Church History Library.

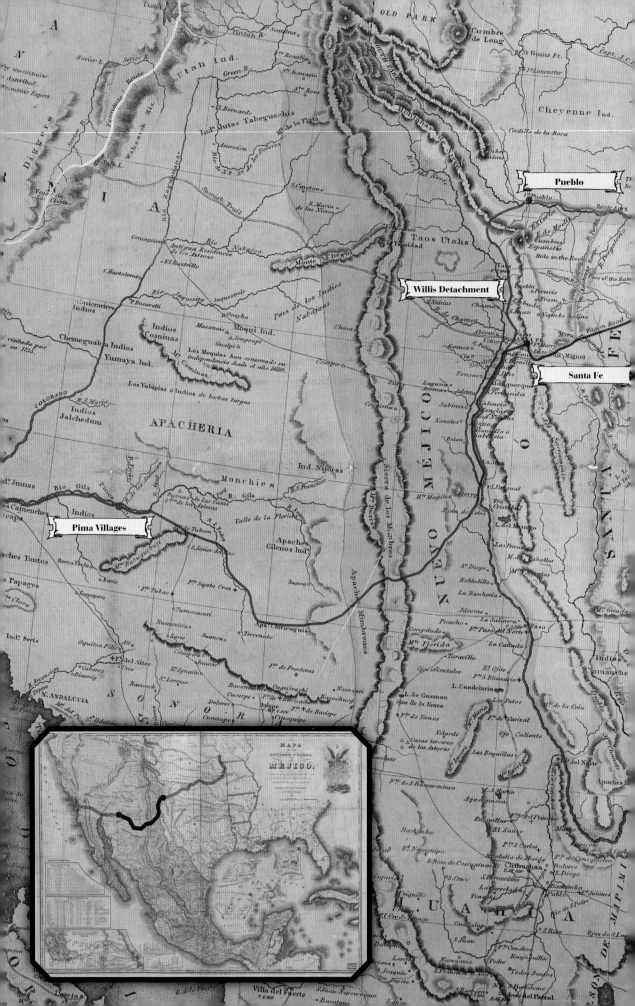

Pueblo

Willis Detachment

Santa Fe

Pima Villages

Chapter Four

SANTA FE TO THE PIMA INDIAN VILLAGES

"None but ourselves will ever know how much we suffered"

By the mid-1820s, Santa Fe was well established as a major trading center for Americans, Mexicans, and Indians. Each year, wagon caravans brought goods overland from Independence, Missouri. The Santa Fe trade was quite lucrative for the traders and stimulated the growth of what was once a sleepy little town. In the 1840s, Santa Fe was caught in the middle of the border dispute between Mexico and the Republic of Texas.[1] Consequently, American trade was prohibited by the Mexican government, prompting Secretary of War William L. Marcy to order General Kearny to take Santa Fe as a first step in the conquest of New Mexico and Upper California. After capturing Santa Fe—and, by extension, the province of New Mexico—without a fight, Kearny hastily pressed on to California, leaving his wagons for the Mormon Battalion to transport west. While at La Joya, 120 miles from Santa Fe, Kearny received word of the death of Captain James Allen. He then appointed Lieutenant Colonel Philip St. George Cooke as Allen's successor with instructions to return to Santa Fe and await the arrival of the Battalion.[2]

Following a weeklong layover in Santa Fe, the Battalion continued its march on October 19 under its new commander. Born in Leesburg, Virginia, in 1809, Cooke was an experienced soldier, having graduated from the United States Military Academy at West Point and having served in the Black Hawk War in Illinois. As one of Kearny's most trusted officers, Cooke was well prepared to lead the Mormon Battalion. The initial days of travel out of Santa Fe proved difficult as the group was compelled to push wagons over deep, sandy terrain, again with an inadequate supply of water and provisions.

Shortly after the Battalion arrived in Santa Fe, Cooke received orders to take sixty days' rations and open a "wagon road to the Pacific."[3] The Battalion had followed well-established trails from Fort Leavenworth to Santa Fe; that all changed on the next leg of the march. On September 25, weeks before the Mormon Battalion arrived in the city,

Kearny and roughly three hundred troops hastily left Santa Fe for Upper California, following the Rio Grande River, also known as the Rio del Norte. To secure American control of Upper California, Kearny wanted to cover the distance to the Pacific in the shortest possible time, so he left his wagons and much of his supplies behind for Cooke and the Battalion to bring west. Cooke assumed command of the Battalion nearly three weeks later and, along with Kearny's thirty wagons and supplies, made preparations for the march west. He gathered what rations were available, including "flour, sugar, and coffee, and salt; thirty [days] of salt pork, and twenty of soap," along with three mule wagons and six ox wagons for each company.[4]

Lieutenant Colonel Philip St. George Cooke (1809–1895) assumed command of the Mormon Battalion in October 1846 and led them on their march from Santa Fe to the Pacific coast. (Courtesy of National Archives.)

In preparing to retrace Kearny's southern route along the Rio Grande River, Cooke enlisted the service of several non-Mormon scouts—often referred to as "pilots" by Battalion diarists—to counter the unreliable maps of the region west of the river. The primary scouts included mountain man Pauline Weaver; Philip Thompson; Stephen Foster, Yale alumni and chief Spanish translator for the remainder of the march; Antoine Leroux, chief scout and the scout most familiar with the Gila Valley; and Jean-Baptiste Charbonneau, son of Sacagawea and Toussaint Charbonneau of Lewis and Clark fame.[5] They functioned as surveyors of the landscape in advance of the Battalion to locate water sources and advise Cooke regarding the most practical routes and campsites. While the scouts often frustrated Cooke by not returning in a timely manner and failing to find water, they were essential in determining the route for the Battalion through endless miles of unfamiliar and rugged territory.

From the outset, Cooke complained that the Battalion was undisciplined and "much worn by travelling on foot, and marching from Nauvoo" and that Battalion soldiers lacked the know-how to care for their animals. Daniel Tyler placed the blame for their worn-out condition squarely on Lieutenant Andrew Jackson Smith and fellow Mormon Adjutant George P. Dykes for their "foolish and unnecessary" forced marches from Leavenworth to Santa Fe, "which utterly broke down both men and beasts, and was the prime cause of the greater part of the sickness" so prevalent among the group.[6] In contrast, Cooke's leadership style and wise judgment in establishing the traveling tempo was soon recognized and appreciated. Private James A. Scott summed up the feelings of many of the Mormon soldiers when he noted, "Since Col. Cooke has had the command, we march moderately, camp early, & everything is done up order[ly]."[7]

Understandably, Colonel Cooke was concerned about the families and laundresses traveling with the Battalion. He was fully aware of the potential for combat with the Mexicans and knew that the strenuous nature of marching across a desert and cutting a wagon road was no place for women and children from a military perspective. Cooke ordered all women and children to Pueblo with the aforementioned Brown detachment the day before leaving Santa Fe, although "five wives of officers were reluctantly allowed to accompany the march, but furnished their own transportation."[8] Ironically, removing the women and children from the picture did not improve the distance or speed of the march by the Battalion.

Cooke and his Mormon Battalion left Santa Fe and for three weeks followed the Rio Grande River south. Within a few days Cooke ordered rations reduced, to the great concern of the men. Henry Standage noted, "we are now on ¾ rations and if reduced so soon what will we be obliged to do ere we reach San Diego."[9] In addition to inadequate rations, the men struggled with the hilly and sandy topography along the banks of the Rio Grande. Regularly wading through the tributaries of the river with sand in their shoes inflicted severe pain on the men's feet. James S. Brown recalled the emotional as well as physical stress on the men at the time. "The men marched along, their clothes wet, and their thick soled cowhide army shoes partly filled with sand—the chaffing and galling of the flesh without and the gnawing and grinding of the stomach within defied the mind to dwell upon any one subject for long at a time."[10]

The numerous Mexican villages in close proximity to the Rio Grande River provided opportunities for the Mormons to interact with unfamiliar cultures and people. They found the locals' lack of attire peculiar. Daniel Tyler observed that "many of the men were as nude as when born, except a breech-clout, or, as Colonel Cooke has it, 'center-clothing,' tied around the loins."[11] The Mexicans were anxious to sell their goods at inflated prices to travelers. Apples, grapes, corn, and wine were available to those willing to part with their meager funds. Private Robert S. Bliss wrote: "Marched ten or twelve miles through almost continuous town of Spaniards and Indians. Saw many beautiful farms and vineyards with peach and apple orchards."[12] The local residents were so enthralled at the sight of the women traveling with the Battalion that William Coray recorded they "would crowd us in such multitudes that I could hardly press my way through."[13]

Despite their heavy use, the roads along the Rio Grande were terrible. Remaining close to the river guaranteed a water source, but the sandy river plain was not conducive to wagon traffic. At times the Battalion struggled to cover more than a mile or two an

George P. Dykes (1814–1888) served as adjutant and was accused of wearing out both men and pack animals for what some believed to be forced marches. (Courtesy of International Society Daughters of Utah Pioneers, Salt Lake City.)

hour as they rallied together to push wagons. Their shoes "became so dry and hard that walking was very painful and difficult, and our feet became raw. . . . as we tramped on through the sands we became so weak it was almost impossible to keep our ankles from striking together as we walked, and our hard and dry shoetops would cut our ankles till the blood came."[14]

Colonel Cooke knew firsthand the stress and fatigue his troops were under. In late October "a sand hill reaching the river bank was encountered; two hours, with teams doubled, and twenty men to a wagon, were required to reach its top,—only three of four hundred paces." The men employed ropes to assist the teams in dragging the

Sketch created in 1878 of the route taken by the Mormon Battalion from the Rio Grande to the Pima Indian villages on the Gila River. (Courtesy of Church History Library.)

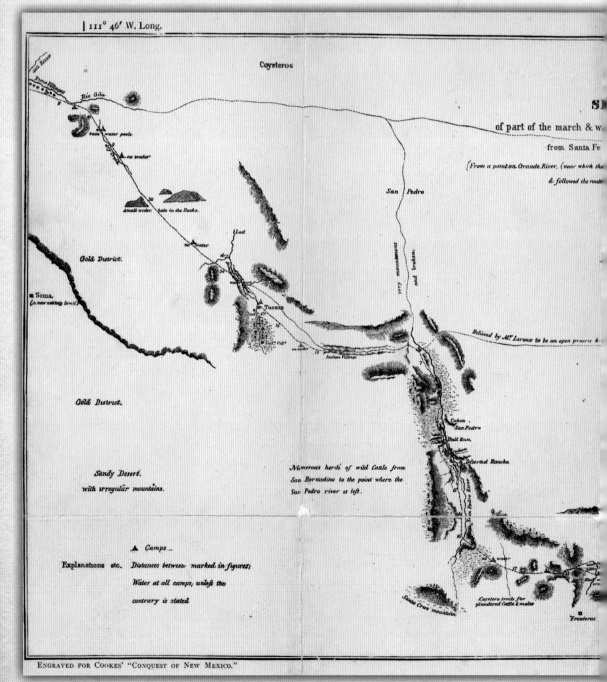

ENGRAVED FOR COOKES' "CONQUEST OF NEW MEXICO."

wagons through the sand. Even the locals were sympathetic to the soldiers' plight and furnished the Battalion with "spades and large hoes" and "worked with them unasked." Cooke was quick to admit that "it was a difficult job."[15] Things would only get worse in the coming days and weeks.

A few weeks earlier, General Kearny and his two companies of dragoons left the Rio Grande near Elephant Butte and headed due west for the Gila River. Recognizing that the road was too difficult for wagons to navigate and the arid environs could not sustain the large number of men and animals traveling with the Battalion, Kearny posted a sign for Cooke that read "Mormon

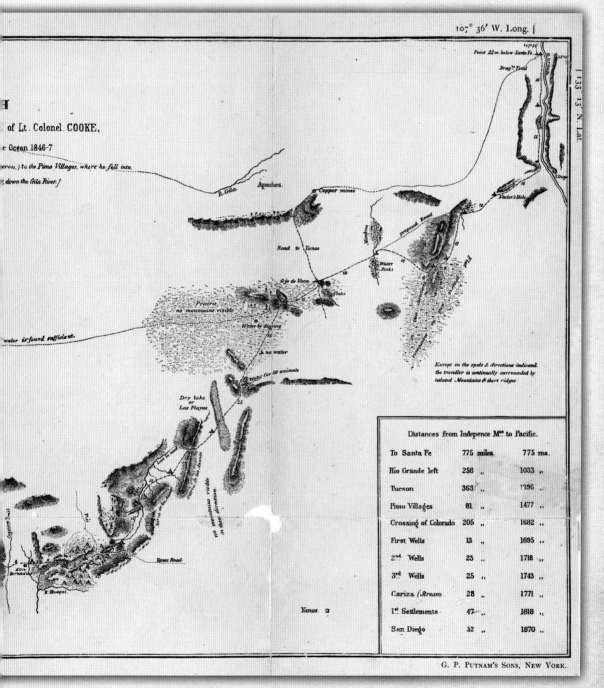

Trail." Clarification of Kearny's sign was relayed to Cooke by Leroux, who explained that Kearny recommended the Mormon Battalion continue southwest along the Rio Grande River for another seventy or eighty miles before cutting west to the San Pedro River.

In the first week of November, two events impacted the morale of the Battalion members. First, James Hampton of Company A died suddenly, possibly from a heart ailment. Time and resources did not allow for immediate burial, so "he was placed in a wagon and carried to our next camping place, where he was buried, a lone stranger in a strange land."[16] Hampton's passing brought the Battalion death toll to eight, including those in the Fort Pueblo detachments. The same day, Cooke ordered a further reduction in rations. This did not sit well with the men, because the new ration allotment failed to provide adequate nourishment to sustain the daily exertion of the march. Again, the sandy roads prevented the men from advancing much more than a mile an hour, and Cooke realized that the teams could not withstand many more consecutive days of travel. After seventeen straight days of marching since leaving Santa Fe, Cooke mercifully declared a welcome day of rest on November 5.

The Battalion soldiers pushed their bodies to the limit on a daily basis. To make even minimal progress on the poor roads through deep sand, all of the soldiers had to spend hours of pushing wagons one at a time as well as pulling the wagons with ropes. Pack mules gave out and were so exhausted that they were not even secured at night, being too tired to wander off. This was ground "where no wagons . . . before had made a track," and the intense labor involved discouraged the men enough that they tried to convince Cooke to abandon all of the wagons; he refused.[17] With so many soldiers in a weakened condition, rumors began to circulate that another group would be detached and sent to Pueblo.

The rumor became fact near Elephant Butte when the third and final detachment was dismissed from the Battalion on November 10. Under the command of Lieutenant William W. Willis, the group of nearly sixty men and one laundress was instructed to "proceed to Santa Fe and report for instructions as to his winter quarters or further movement."[18] Within two days, three additional men were dispatched by Cooke to catch up with Willis. Losing the Willis detachment now reduced the Battalion members by roughly 40 percent from its peak of four hundred and ninety-six at Fort Leavenworth. The loss of yet another portion of the unit was upsetting, and some questioned Cooke's foresight in planning for the teams and provisions. Henry Standage noted, "This does in reality make solemn times for us, so many divisions taking place."[19] Upon reaching Santa Fe, Willis reported to Colonel Sterling Price, the Mormons' former Missouri nemesis. Exhibiting no compassion, Price refused to allow the Willis detachment to winter in Santa

Fe; instead, he ordered Willis and his soldiers to continue three hundred more miles to Pueblo despite the onset of winter. Most of the detachment reached Pueblo on December 20. A dozen men lagged behind and did not arrive until mid-January 1847—short one man, William Coleman, who died en route.[20]

Cooke used this third detachment as an opportunity to shed some cumbersome weight for his journey ahead; he sent a wagon full of supplies with Willis's group, including "many tents, and camp kettles . . . and all the upright poles." Tent poles were resourcefully replaced by muskets, expanding the sleeping capacity of the tents "in which ten men were accommodated."[21] The remaining equipment and provisions were rearranged more efficiently in an effort to lighten the wagon loads for better maneuverability.

Already stressed, the physical condition of the men declined even more quickly after they left the Rio Grande River on November 13 and veered westward. Thirst, hunger, warm temperatures, and the strains of constantly pushing wagons through deep sand all took a relentless toll on the group. There was no longer immediate access to water, and food became so scarce that Henry Standage recorded "that the Col. has ordered an old white ox to be killed." The dilapidated beast was "really the poorest beef that can be imagined and not only is there a lack of fat, but it is covered with sores caused by the blows received from day to day in order to get the poor thing through the deep sands. Some complain a little at this kind of meat, but if we do not eat mule meat before we receive a plenty I should be glad."[22] Many simply refused to eat the grotesque jellylike meat.

Aside from the discomfort of hunger pains and physical exhaustion caused by scarce rations, the noxious desert vegetation became a source of frustration and pain. Private Guy M. Keysor recorded, "The shrubbery covering these hills are mostly green & beautiful. They are the most all strangers to me especially by name but by sight they familiarize themselves much faster than I would wish them to especially the acquaintance they scrape with my legs every day not only keeps my cloth[e]s in rags but often penetrates the skin."[23]

On November 20 Cooke's scouts reported that there was no viable trail for the Battalion to continue their westward course of travel. Seeking the advice of locals, Cooke had a fire built as a distress signal that summoned nearby Mexican traders and Apache Indians. They counseled Cooke to divert his march south to Janos, an established trade route connecting abandoned copper mines in southern New Mexico to Janos in northern Sonora. Cooke became convinced that the route to Janos was his only real option, and upon reaching the settlement the Battalion could replenish supplies and obtain

Guy M. Keysor (1816–1885) was a member of Company B and wrote of the harsh environs encountered by the soldiers as they cut a new wagon road across current-day New Mexico and Arizona. (Courtesy of International Society Daughters of Utah Pioneers, Salt Lake City.)

Levi W. Hancock (1803–1882) was among the older members of the Mormon Battalion and served as musician. Hancock was considered the ecclesiastical leader of the men and encouraged the men to pray in an effort to change Cooke's mind from traveling south toward Mexico. (Courtesy of Church History Library.)

fresh teams. The decision so alarmed Levi W. Hancock, the soldiers' spiritual leader, that he, along with David Pettigrew and William Hyde, visited the tent of every Battalion member that evening asking the men to "pray to the Lord to change the Colonel's mind."[24]

In the morning, the men "struck our tents and took up the line of march directly south and continued this course nearly two miles," explained William Hyde, "when the Col became dissatisfied with the course and swore he would continue it no further, we then left the Copper mine road and took up a line of march directly west."[25] What prompted Cooke's sudden change of mind is not completely clear. From the perspective of most soldiers it was undoubtedly divine intervention in answer to the fervent prayers they had offered a few hours earlier. According to Henry Standage, once Colonel Cooke realized they were headed southeast instead of west, he "said he started to go to San Diego, Upper California and he meant to go the near way and then ordered the Command to turn west leaving the well beaten road for the trackless desert."[26] In his report to Kearny, Cooke explained that he had "reluctantly assented" to take the Janos road, and after a mile or two it was clear that the road's "general direction was very different from their [traders and Apaches] representations."[27] In the coming weeks, the decision to abandon the Janos route had a great impact on the men, as they now began the arduous task of cutting a new wagon road through completely uncharted country. To this point they had followed established roads, but now they had to make their own. Cooke's orders to have the Mormon Battalion build a wagon road to the Pacific now depended on one critical resource—water. The pressure on the scouts became intense—if dependable water sources could not be found, the entire effort became an exercise in futility.

For two full days the men marched without water; some experienced a "deceptive mirage . . . constantly before us, seeming to keep the same distance off; sometimes it looked like a river, at other like a sea or lake."[28] In this desperate situation, the soldiers went to extreme lengths to "get some little to assuage their thirst, some sucking water through quills, as it seeped from the crack in the rocks."[29] James S. Brown described his thirst as so intense that "it did not seem possible that I could live till morning." Many of the men looked "like death, their mouths black, their eyes sunken till it was difficult to recognize them" and it appeared that "the monster death were close at hand."[30] This dearth of water constantly plagued the Battalion through much of its march to the Pacific.

Some of the most challenging days on this leg of the journey involved the passage over the Guadalupe Mountains, where peaks exceeded six thousand feet. The steep descent over the rugged terrain required the men to transfer supplies from the wagons to the pack animals, then laboriously lower the empty wagons one by one down canyons with ropes. A number of the wagons were damaged in the process and required maintenance before they could move forward. Henry Bigler described the punishing labor that was often required, using "pick-axe and crow-bar . . . to clear the most feasible road down by chopping away the shrubbery and brush and removing that and the rocks."[31] He also reflected on his commander's determination, noting, "I think no other man but Cooke would ever have attempted to cross such a place, but he seemed to have the spirit and energy of a Bonypart."[32]

Although the Battalion marched in a desert environment, it was winter; the temperature now dropped, particularly at night, and the rations were so scant and poor that the malnourished men were forced to broaden their ideas of acceptable food. Strips of rawhide were boiled for soup, and it became routine to eat their weary and ailing oxen, as noted by Henry Standage: "We have been eating work Oxen for some time, working the Oxen as long as they could be made to go and then killing them for the command. The men are literally worn out and eating much meat as we do now, I believe makes men sluggish and feel more like worn out beings through

One of the most difficult obstacles encountered by the Battalion was the Guadalupe Mountains. The rugged terrain required wagons to be offloaded and lowered down canyons by rope. (Courtesy of the Library of Congress.)

diseased cattle."[33] As oxen grew too weak to pull the wagons they were slaughtered, and every scrap was divided among the men. James S. Brown wrote that this included "the hide, intestines—all was eaten; even the tender of soft edges of the hoofs and horns would be roasted, and gnawed at so long as a human being possibly could draw subsistence therefrom. Many times we were without water to wash the offal. The bones would be carried along, broken up, and boiled and re-boiled."[34]

After overcoming the obstacles of the Guadalupe Mountains, on December 2 the Battalion arrived at an abandoned ranch in the San Bernardino Valley in what is today northern Mexico, just south of the New Mexico–Arizona border. The Apache Indians had chased Mexican settlers and military units out of the valley more than a decade earlier and had scattered herds of cattle in the process. The Battalion remained at the ranch to wash clothes, re-cuperate, and trade with two dozen Apache Indians. A number of wild cattle still roamed the vicinity and provided the Battalion with prime meat, a stark contrast to the unappetizing oxen of the preceding days. However, this additional food fell short in satisfy-ing Henry G. Boyle, who wrote, "We feel hungry all the time, we never get enough."[35] While the ranch offered a degree of relief from the daily strains of the march, it was short-lived; within two days, Cooke led the Battalion northwest toward the San Pedro River.

The men reached the San Pedro, a tributary of the Gila run-ning north-south, on December 9 and found plentiful resources in the form of cattle, horses, antelope, and fish, as well as grass for the teams to feed on and timber for fire. On December 11, the re-markable number of wild cattle became a dangerous threat to the command when the cattle charged at the Battalion in what came to be known as the "Battle of the Bulls." Accounts differ slightly as to what caused the frightening stampede. Some sources claim the men were marching and startled a herd of wild bulls, while others believed the bulls were spooked by a number of Battalion hunters.[36] Whatever the case, dozens of aggressive bulls charged the soldiers, and mayhem ensued as men frantically ran for cover and began discharging their guns. Daniel Tyler recalled that some "climbed upon the wheels of the wagons," others "climbed up in small trees," and a number simply "threw themselves down and al-lowed the beasts to run over them."[37] A few Battalion members were injured. Private Amos Cox was thrown ten feet in the air and gored in the thigh; Sergeant Albert Smith was trampled by a bull; and three mules were gruesomely gored to death, one of which was spotted "with entrails hanging a foot below his body." The bulls were described as "dareing & Savage as tigers" and "very hard to kill; they would run off with a half dozen balls in them unless they were shot in the heart."[38]

In amazement, Colonel Cooke described the calm yet seemingly reckless action taken by Corporal Lafayette Frost as a bull charged toward him: "I . . . saw an immense coal black bull charge on Corporal Frost of Company A; he stood his ground, while the animal rushed right on for one hundred yards. I was close by, and believed the man in great danger to his life, and spoke to him; he aimed his musket very deliberately, and only fired when the beast was within ten paces, and it fell headlong almost at his feet."[39] Cooke purportedly stated that Frost was "one of the bravest men he ever saw" but that "he wanted no farther proofs of his courage."[40] When the dust settled, a good number of dead bulls littered the

landscape, but aside from the few injuries and loss of some mules, the command walked away unscathed.

The following day, while marching northwest from the San Pedro toward the Santa Cruz River, the threat of combat became a reality for the first time since the Battalion left Council Bluffs in July. Advance scout Antoine Leroux brought Cooke word that a Mexican garrison numbering two hundred strong was stationed less than forty miles ahead in Tucson. Undaunted by the threat, Cooke drilled his men in battle tactics and formations, inspected arms, and issued twenty-eight rounds of ammunition to each man for target practice. Four scouts were dispatched by Cooke to negotiate the peaceful passage of the Battalion through Tucson, it being the direct route and an opportunity to restock provisions. William Coray recounted that a short time later the Battalion was "met by

The Mormon Battalion was stampeded by wild bulls in an event that became known as the "Battle of the Bulls" on December 11, 1846, along the San Pedro River. Numerous soldiers sustained injuries and several pack mules were killed. (Courtesy of Church History Library.)

Nathaniel V. Jones (1822–1863) was a sergeant in Company D and later served missions to India and England. In 1856, he was selected by Brigham Young to head up a lead mining venture in the Las Vegas area. (Courtesy of Church History Library.)

seven dragoons (Mexican) from the Garrison. One of them wanted to know our intentions, whether it was to kill, destroy and take prisoners, or to pass through peaceably, to which the Lt. Col. replied that it was to pass through in peace, that they did not come to make war on Sonora . . . but wished to trade with them for provisions and mules as we were quite destitute."[41] Cooke pushed on and upon learning that one of his scouts, Stephen Foster, had been taken prisoner by the Mexican troops, he took three Mexican soldiers as hostages in retaliation.

Colonel Cooke received notice that he must go around the city or fight but paid no attention to the request. Albert Smith noted that the men were "all ordered to load our Gons [guns] & fix barnet [bayonets] & prepare for A fite if nessary."[42] As the Battalion soldiers approached Tucson, Nathaniel V. Jones recorded meeting "several men . . . who tried to have us pass around the fort, but the colonel pushed on with double speed until we came to the town, when upon our arrival, the soldiers fled and many of the inhabitants with them taking all their public arms etc. with them." With the situation defused, Cooke marched his command through town on December 16, set up camp on the west side, and seized some bushels of wheat that were used to feed his men and animals. According to Jones, a number of the men also "purchase[d] from the inhabitants . . . a few beans and a little flour by exchanging our clothes for it."[43]

The next day the looming reality of combat returned when Cooke assembled about fifty volunteers to pursue the fleeing Mexican garrison and possibly seize their artillery and mules. One of the volunteers, William Coray, became convinced that a battle was inevitable and his thoughts turned to his wife, Melissa Coray, one of four women still traveling with the Mormon Battalion. "I could not help thinking of Mrs. Coray while I was in ranks wondering what she would do if the battle commenced, but this was one of the places where a trust in God was necessary to reconciliation."[44] The reconnaissance was aborted, according to assistant surgeon George B. Sanderson, after Cooke "began to reflect seriously his hazardous undertaking and wisely called a council of war" that determined to return to Tucson.[45]

Between Tucson and the Pima Indian villages on the Gila River, the Battalion faced seventy miles of parched desert. The soldiers left Tucson on December 18 unaware of the agonizing miles ahead with no water and the necessity of once again marching through heavy sand. This time the situation was more severe than in November. They followed the Santa Cruz River, but it sank underground north of Tucson. Some of the men went searching for water late that night and found very little. The following day the condition of the men worsened, and Guy M. Keysor wrote that they "suffered very much for the want of water, and some might have perished, if we had not found one or two mud-holes about sundown. These holes afforded a swallow to each man—being permitted only to lay down and lap it like a dog, or, in other words, to take what we could drink at once." This method of prostrating their bodies to the earth, lapping up water, and preventing any dipping of canteens or hands was strictly enforced. This allowed the maximum number possible to receive a taste. Keysor further explained that some of the desperate men who attempted to return to the mud holes that night "lost their way and wandered about all night," and that the resilient mules built to withstand harsh conditions "bellowed piteously all night."[46] Those who were fortunate enough to receive a "little water" savored it and "sipped [it] down as readily as if it had been choice wine."[47]

The constant thirst brought many of the men to their breaking point. For Henry G. Boyle, the months of arduous, backbreaking work seemed to culminate during this unforgiving stretch of desert, making him feel weakened "from hunger and thirst; also from the fatigue of our long marches, camp duty, etc. None but ourselves will ever know how much we suffered."[48] William Hyde recalled that whenever water was located, the soldiers hurried to the "waters edge and after drinking and resting and again drinking and resting and continuing this operation for a time we succeeded in quenching our thirst. But on arising from the ground we felt that we were not much less than ninety and nine years old."[49]

These extreme conditions resulted in some creative remedies for quenching their thirst. James S. Brown recounted that they "would chew a buck-shot or two to induce moisture" on their

The Battalion soldiers likely passed the Mission San Xavier Del Bac, located nine miles south of Tucson, in mid-December 1846. (Charles L. Camp Collection of Stereographs, Bancroft Library.)

parched tongues.[50] Melissa Coray carried a smooth stone in her pocket and placed it in her mouth to generate saliva during the long marches without water.[51] William Hyde described how the men attempted to make the filthy water from the mud holes more palatable by mixing "a little flour in some, but the water was so thick with mud that it would admit but a small portion of flour . . . [and] was like eating clay."[52]

After enduring the almost waterless seventy miles between Tucson and the Pima Indian villages, Colonel Cooke was heard to say, "Any other company under like circumstances would have mutinized." He further stated "that had he known the situation of the desert, he would not have ventured upon it as he had on any account."[53] From such a seasoned military officer this was a great compliment, considering that he once viewed the Battalion as merely a group of ragtag volunteers. During the course of the march from Santa Fe, the actions of the Mormons erased Cooke's initial skepticism of their abilities.

Cooke and his Battalion finally staggered into the Pima Indian villages along the Gila River on December 22, where they were received warmly. Even before their arrival, nearly two hundred Pimas came to trade with the unit. Henry Standage noted that they brought "meal, corn, beans, dried pumpkins, and watermelons, which they readily exchanged for old shirts, &c. These Indians appear glad to see us, many of them running and taking us by the hand."[54] The Pimas and the Mormon soldiers engaged in friendly trade over the next two days, and at one point it was estimated that there were a thousand Indians in camp. The Battalion relished in the readily available watermelon, molasses, pumpkins, cornmeal,

Lithograph of Pima and Maricopa Indians, circa 1846, by W. H. Emory. The Mormon Battalion arrived at the Pima Indian villages on December 22, 1846, and received supplies and assistance from these tribes located on the Gila River. (Courtesy of Bancroft Library, UC Berkeley.)

PIMOS & COCO MARICOPAS INDIANS

and beans. Upon reaching the Gila River, the Battalion rejoined the route taken by General Kearny. The Battalion's fifty-day, five-hundred-mile detour from the Rio Grande to the Gila River formed part of what became known as Cooke's Wagon Road.

On Christmas morning, the command struck their tents and rolled out of the Pima villages westward bound. William Hyde observed, "This is rather a strange Christmas to me. My situation with my family in days gone by was called to mind, and contrasted with my present situation on the sandy deserts through which pass the Gila and Colorado Rivers; growing faint and weary for want of those comforts which nature requires to give strength and vigor to the body, and also suffering much at times for the want of water, but still pressing forward with parched lips, scalded shoulders, weary limbs, blistered feet, worn out shoes and ragged clothes; but with me the prospect of my present toils, cheers me on."[55]

The two grueling months since leaving Santa Fe brought the Mormon Battalion more than eight hundred miles closer to the Pacific. Pushing wagons through deep sand, crossing the Guadalupe Mountains, enduring a violent stampede, preparing to engage in combat on at least two occasions, enduring a constant shortage of rations, and marching days without water pushed the men to their physical and emotional limits. Cooke's Wagon Road immediately linked the roads from Mexico and Santa Fe with Tucson and the Gila, significantly improving transportation and commerce in the region. The experiences of this leg of the journey built upon those encountered from Fort Leavenworth to Santa Fe, hardening the resolve of the men and instilling greater confidence to carry on as they continued southwest across the desert. Colonel Cooke provided the solid leadership and stability the Battalion lacked earlier in its journey. The soldiers' brief stop in the Pima villages gave them a few days to replenish supplies as well as rest and recuperate before following Kearny's track in their final push to the coast, a part of the journey that promised to try their endurance in every way.

Endnotes

1. For more on Santa Fe, see Stephen G. Hyslop, *Bound for Santa Fe: The Road to New Mexico and the American Conquest, 1806–1848* (Norman, OK: Oklahoma University Press, 2002).

2. Cooke, *The Conquest of New Mexico and California*, 77–78. News of Allen's death came on October 2; Cooke was appointed to assume command over the Mormon Battalion that evening and set out for Santa Fe the next morning.

3. Cooke, *The Conquest of New Mexico and California*, 86.

4. Manuscript History of the Mormon Battalion, 19 October 1846, Church History Library.

5. Fleek, *History May Be Searched in Vain*, 241.

6. Tyler, *A Concise History of the Mormon Battalion*, 174.

7. James A. Scott, Journal, 27 October 1846, Church History Library.

8. Cooke, *The Conquest of New Mexico and California*, 91–92. The women included Lydia Hunter, Phebe Brown, Melissa Coray, Sophia Gribble (Tubbs), and Susan Davis. Gribble retreated to Pueblo in November with the Willis detachment and did not make it to the Pacific.

9. Standage, Journal, 21 October 1846, in Golder, ed., *The March of the Mormon Battalion*, 139.

10. James S. Brown, *Life of a Pioneer: Being the Autobiography of James S. Brown* (Salt Lake City: Geo. Q. Cannon & Sons, 1900), 43–44.

11. Tyler, *A Concise History of the Mormon Battalion*, 178.

12. Bliss, Diary, 27 October 1846, Church History Library.

13. William Coray, 25 October 1846, as quoted in Manuscript History of the Mormon Battalion, Church History Library.

14. Brown, *Life of a Pioneer*, 46.

15. Cooke, *The Conquest of New Mexico and California*, 99.

16. Tyler, *A Concise History of the Mormon Battalion*, 186.

17. Bliss, Diary, 7 November 1846, Church History Library.

18. Orders, No. 16, 10 November 1846, as quoted in the Manuscript History of the Mormon Battalion, Church History Library; 21 December 1846, Manuscript History of the Mormon Battalion. The total number comprising the Willis detachment varies in extant sources from fifty-five to fifty-seven individuals.

19. Standage, 10 November 1846, in Golder, ed., *The March of the Mormon Battalion*, 182–183.

20. Manuscript History of the Mormon Battalion, 2 December 1846, Church History Library; Ricketts, *The Mormon Battalion: U.S. Army of the West*, 242.

21. Hamilton Gardner, ed., "Report of Lieut. Col. P. St. George Cooke of His March from Santa Fe, New Mexico, to San Diego, Upper California," *Utah Historical Quarterly* 22 (January 1954), 21.

22. Standage, 15 November 1846, in Golder, ed., *The March of the Mormon Battalion*, 184.

23. Guy M. Keysor, Journal, 6 November 1846, Church History Library.

24. Manuscript History of the Mormon Battalion, 20 November 1846, Church History Library; Tyler, 206.

25. William Hyde, Journal, 21 November 1846, Church History Library; Hyde, *The Private Journal of William Hyde*, 31.

26. Standage, 21 November 1846, in Golder, ed., *The March of the Mormon Battalion*, 186.

27. "Report of Lieut. Col. P. St. George Cooke," in Gardner, ed., 23.

28. Tyler, *A Concise History of the Mormon Battalion*, 209.

29. Standage, 23 November 1846, in Golder, ed., *The March of the Mormon Battalion*, 186–187.

30. Brown, *Life of a Pioneer*, 49.

31. Ibid., 54.

32. Gudde, *Bigler's Chronicle of the West*, 29.

33. Standage, 30 November 1846, in Golder, ed., *The March of the Mormon Battalion*, 189.

34. Brown, *Life of a Pioneer*, 48.

35. Henry G. Boyle, Reminiscences and Diaries, 3 December 1846, Church History Library.

36. For varying accounts, compare the 11 December entries in the journals of Guy M. Keysor, William Coray, Robert S. Bliss, and Tyler, 218.

37. Tyler, *A Concise History of the Mormon Battalion*, 219.

38. Boyle, 11 December 1846, Church History Library; Manuscript History of the Mormon Battalion, 11 December 1846, Church History Library.

39. In "Public Documents Printed by Order of the Senate of the United States during a Special Session Begun and Held at the City of Washington, March 5, 1849"

(Washington, DC: Union Office, 1849), 37; see also Cooke, 146.

40 Tyler, *A Concise History of the Mormon Battalion*, 220; Manuscript History of the Mormon Battalion, 11 December 1846, Church History Library.

41 William Coray, Journal, 14 December 1846, as quoted in Ricketts, *The Mormon Battalion: U.S. Army of the West*, 95.

42 Albert Smith, Reminiscences and Journal, 16 December 1846, Church History Library.

43 Nathaniel Vary Jones, Journal, typescript, 15 December 1846, Church History Library.

44 William Coray, Journal, 17 December 1846, as quoted in Ricketts, *The Mormon Battalion: U.S. Army of the West*, 100.

45 George B. Sanderson, Journal, 17 December 1846, as quoted in Fleek, *History May Be Searched in Vain*, 293.

46 Keysor, Journal, 19 December 1846, Church History Library.

47 Hyde, Journal, 19 December 1846, Church History Library; Hyde, *The Private Journal of William Hyde*, 35.

48 Boyle, 19 December 1846, Church History Library.

49 Hyde, Journal, 20 December 1846, Church History Library; Hyde, *The Private Journal of William Hyde*, 35.

50 Brown, *Life of a Pioneer*, 64.

51 Norma Baldwin Ricketts, *Melissa's Journey with the Mormon Battalion: The Western Odyssey of Melissa Burton Coray, 1846–1848* (Salt Lake City: Daughters of Utah Pioneers, 1994), 49.

52 Hyde, Journal, 20 December 1846, Church History Library; Hyde, *The Private Journal of William Hyde*, 35-36.

53 Ibid.

54 Standage, 21 December 1846, in Golder, ed., *The March of the Mormon Battalion*, 198.

55 Hyde, Journal, *The Private Journal of William Hyde*, 36.

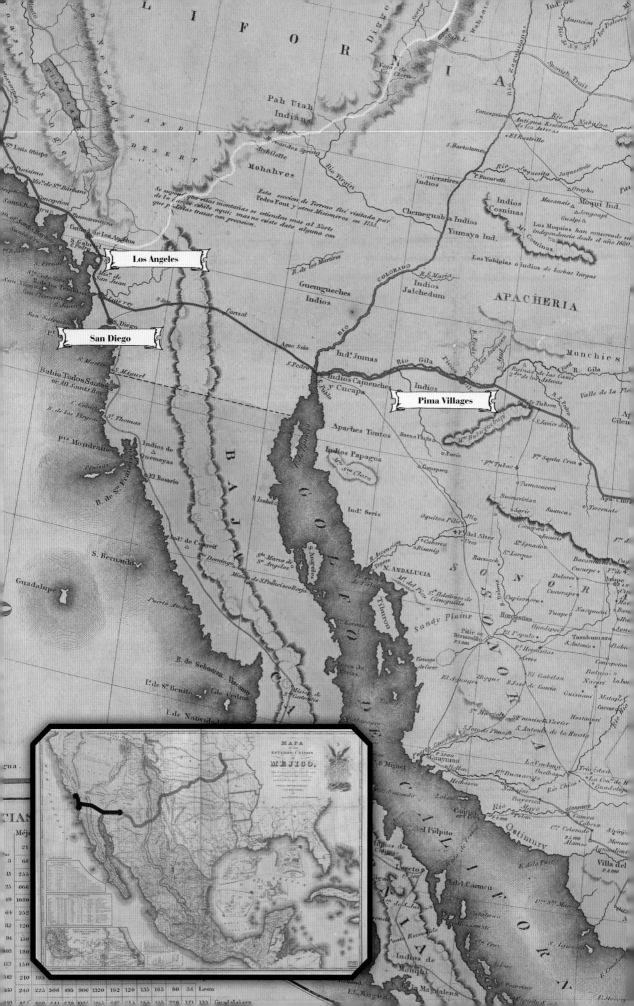

Los Angeles

San Diego

Pima Villages

Chapter Five

PIMA VILLAGES TO THE PACIFIC

"Nothing could have saved our lives but the unseen hand of Almighty God"

As the soldiers of the Mormon Battalion left the Pima villages on Christmas day, they began the last stretch of their march to the Pacific. News about conditions on the coast was picked up as they encountered passing travelers. On December 28, Samuel H. Rogers recorded, "Last night two men came into camp from California. General Kearny has given them passports to Sonora. They reported a Skirmish between Kearny and the Californios in which he gained the victory. They also report a quarrel between Two of the leading Mexican Generals and that the people of California are fleeing from there. This morning an express was Started to Genl Kearny and we resumed our journey. Travelled 18 miles down the [Gila] river."[1]

The report of Kearny's "victory" was anything but accurate. Soon after Kearny's forces arrived in California in early December, they fought a desperate battle at San Pasqual against "Californios" led by Andrés Pico, a wealthy rancher, and his brother Pío, governor of the Mexican province of Alta California. In combat lasting just minutes,

Andrés Pico (1810–1876), brother of Mexican Governor Pío Pico, was a wealthy rancher and one of those who commanded the Mexican forces in Alta California during the Mexican War. His band of "Californios" nearly decimated General Stephen W. Kearny's men in the Battle of San Pasqual. (Courtesy of Bancroft Library, UC Berkeley.)

Famed explorer Kit Carson (1809–1868) was hired as a courier and scout during the Mexican War. He and two others evaded Mexican forces at the Battle of San Pasqual and alerted Robert F. Stockton of the situation. (Courtesy of the Library of Congress.)

Andrés Pico's cavalry, armed with medieval-style lances, decimated Kearny's troops; Kearny himself received two wounds. Although the effects of Kearny's artillery finally forced Pico's forces to withdraw, Kearny's units suffered incredible losses.

Kearny and his men attempted to march to San Diego but were constantly harassed by Pico's cavalry. Finally besieged on what came to be known as Mule Hill, it seemed Kearny and his men faced annihilation, but the famous scout Kit Carson, accompanied by Lieutenant Edward Beale and Beale's Indian "servant," slipped through Mexican lines and made their way to the camp of Commodore Robert F. Stockton for help. Stockton immediately sent a substantial relief force and an additional artillery piece, saving Kearny's forces.[2] Within a month, and after a couple of skirmishes, the forces of Kearny and Stockton had retaken Los Angeles. After January 10 the Pacific coast was, in effect, firmly under American control, while Cooke and the Mormon Battalion were still crossing the Colorado River. Brigham Young's promise that the Mormon Battalion would not face combat with Mexican forces was becoming ever more certain.

While reports of armed conflict between U. S. forces and local Californians must have worried Cooke, his more immediate concern was assuring the survival of his own troops. Beginning with the march from Council Bluffs to Leavenworth, the Battalion had been plagued with an almost constant shortage of provisions. The lack of an adequate diet became especially severe on this last stretch to the Pacific, as the cumulative effects of the long months of marching took its toll on the men. In unfamiliar surroundings and after such a lengthy absence from friends and family, the men's thoughts turned to home. Levi Hancock wrote, "Here we are a handful of as good fellows as ever was in the midst of our enemy and nere Colorado river we see the Mts on the other side and have for two days ago and it is now two days travil to it and I have to say home home sweet home theres no place like home and does me good to see a weed that grows in my own native land."[3] Adding to the stress was the knowledge that their loved ones might well be in adverse conditions without a home at all.

Of course, the longing for home was amplified whenever conditions worsened. Although they had replenished supplies to some extent while at the Pima villages, when a plan to float supplies down the Gila went awry, even those became unavailable; the soldiers were soon back on reduced rations and the animals were fed bark on several occasions. On New Year's Day 1847, Samuel

Rogers recorded the reason for the attempt to float supplies down the Gila: "We are preparing to Send some of the baggage down the river in a boat there by relieving the teams."[4] The next day provisions were loaded into "wagon box" boats on the Gila.[5] Reddick Allred recalled, "In going down the Gila the roads being heavy & the mules weak, the Col. Decided to float two wagon boxes filled with flour down the R. & detailed men for that purpose, which failed because of the many sand bars encountered, which caused the men to abandon their crafts & follow up the command on foot. This was a great disaster—the loss of our flour."[6]

The march from the Pima villages to the confluence of the Gila and Colorado Rivers took thirteen days. While the Gila provided water that the men craved in previous legs of the march, now the lack of provisions began to be keenly felt. On January 6 Cooke noted:

> In five days but fifty-four miles of progress has been made, and after much anxiety the pontoon boat, now first seen, has joined the battalion empty! The experiment proved a failure, and the stores have been landed in several places; but three or four inches of water was to be found on several rapids. Parties with pack mules have been out all the time striving to meet the boat, and recover at least the flour, from its load of two thousand five hundred pounds of provisions and corn. And these have not been heard from![7]

On January 8, just before they reached the Colorado, William Coray recorded that the "men are nearly starving for bread already. There are great prices offered for a morsel. The beef which is the only means for sustenance at this time is of the poorest quality. A man would have been fined in any place but this to have sold such beef. Notwithstanding the intense suffering of the men, there was not much grumbling after all."[8]

By January 11, the Battalion, with the remaining wagons and supplies, had crossed the Colorado. They marched fifteen miles west from the river and, once again, thirst became their enemy. Regarding their food supply, Samuel Rogers wrote, "our rations of flour were now reduced to 8 oz. of flour a day per man."[9] The terrain was so difficult to cross that four wagons were left behind before they reached their next campsite. That evening, the Battalion reached a dry well with a dead wolf in it; the soldiers attempted to dig a new one, which quickly filled with sand. To shore up the sides of the well, Lieutenant George W. Oman requested the use of a washtub belonging to Susan Davis, wife of Captain Daniel C. Davis. According to Daniel Tyler:

The U.S. forces of Commodore Robert F. Stockton (1795–1866) rescued General Stephen W. Kearny and his men from an attack by Andrés Pico in December 1846. (Courtesy of Bancroft Library, UC Berkeley.)

The good lady, who had perhaps brought it all the way from Nauvoo or even farther, could not consent, on any account, to part with it. It was, however, pressed into service, and bored, and sunk in the sand. This proved a failure. Then the bottom was ordered to be knocked out, when it worked better; some water came in, but, alas, for human hopes! the fluid soon disappeared and all seemed lost. . . . [Cooke] ordered a fresh detail to further sink the new well, which was already more than two feet below the old one, with no better prospect. A half hour later all hearts were made glad with the tidings of water deep enough to fill our camp kettles.[10]

Cooke was incredulous. He recalled, "Lieutenant Oman reported to me, to my astonishment, that they were unwilling to give up that valuable article!—upon which our lives seemed to depend. I had it taken."[11] Susan's resistance probably stemmed from the fact that with a washtub, she could earn an income as a laundress—not to mention the fact that she undoubtedly believed the washtub would not be able to shore up the well.

The trouble finding water just added misery to the march. While the four wagons that were left behind were eventually retrieved, others were abandoned during the next day of travel. During this stretch of the journey, mules died constantly and many

Drawing in Levi Hancock's journal of saguaro cactus encountered by the soldiers while traveling along the Gila River. (Courtesy of Church History Library.)

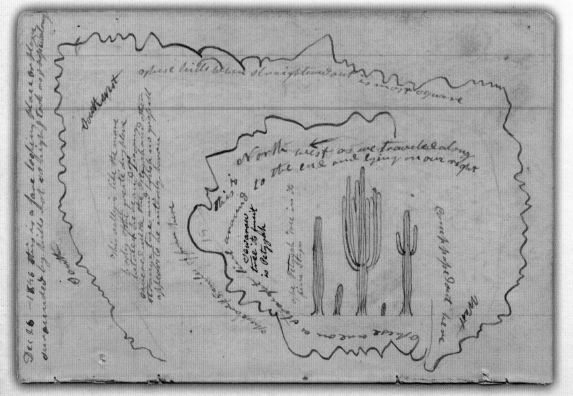

wagons were abandoned. On January 15 at a well site known as Pozo Hondo, Samuel Rogers recorded that some of Kearny's men arrived with an escort of six American Indians and "40 mules and 10 beeves."[12] The following day, William Coray noted that part of the Battalion "did not get to the camp during the day, such was the extreme suffering of the Mormon Battalion. Three days without water and if the fresh beef had not met us nothing could have saved our lives but the unseen hand of Almighty God."[13]

The march from the Yuma crossing of the Colorado River to Jonathan Warner's ranch pushed the soldiers to the limits of their endurance. Henry G. Boyle summarized the difficulty they faced during this part of the march: "We were all weary & fatigued, hungry, nearly naked & barefoot but our burning thirst drowned every other suffering." William Coray described it as "the worst place we had encountered since we left the states."[14]

Even when the soldiers had footwear, it did little to relieve their suffering feet. Levi Hancock recorded, "our shoes are worn out, our torn clothes almost gone. The skins of beeves are used as moccasins. They become hard as sheet iron, and cut the feet. Some go barefoot, and fare no better for <almost> everything has thorns. The ground in many places is full of briars."[15] The condition of the men was recognized by Cooke, who on January 16 wrote, "A great many of my men are wholly without shoes, and use every expedient, such as rawhide moccasins and sandals, and even wrapping their feet in pieces of woolen and cotton cloth."[16]

It was also on January 16 that the Battalion reached Carrizo Creek and fortunately found some water. Daniel Tyler wrote, "Before we arrived at the Cariza [Carrizo Creek], many of the men were so nearly used up from thirst, hunger and fatigue that they were unable to speak until they reached the water or had it brought

This painting by George M. Ottinger depicts the Mormon Battalion gratefully finding water at Carrizo Creek on January 16, 1847, after five days with no reliable water source. (Courtesy of Church History Museum.)

to them. Those who were strongest reported, when they arrived, that they had passed many lying exhausted by the way-side."[17] In order to reach Carrizo Creek, Rogers described the desperate travel on January 16:

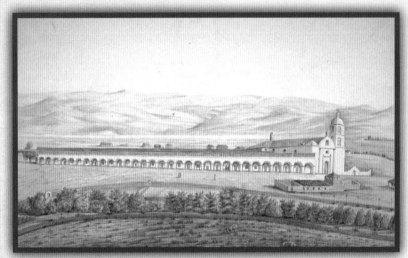

We were aroused at 1:00 a.m. when the march was resumed and continued almost without a halt for 25 miles to the west when we reached running water called the Cariza. This last has been a forced march performed without water. Some of the animals were completely tired out and some killed themselves with drinking.[18]

Levi Hancock described Carrizo Creek as "coming out of the ground a short distance above and loosing aggin itself in the sand not one mile below. I believe the great Missippy would soon be lost in this ocean of sand if it should run out here until it could cut a channel and if I had got to make it my home here I should think it was worse than states prison[.] many of our mules are dead and many are like[ly] to die by hunger and thirst[.] this water was so good to the tast of the mules that they culd drink and die or as bad as dead can not git up[.]"[19] Tyler, echoing the sentiments of William Coray and Henry G. Boyle, claimed the five days of marching previous to reaching Carrizo Creek were "the most trying of any we made, on both men and animals. . . . Language fails to provide adjectives strong enough to describe our situation."[20]

Challenges continued to confront the Battalion. On January 19 David Pettigrew recorded that the Battalion "came to a very narrow pass so much so that the men were obliged to hew the rocks with axes to let the wagons pass through."[21] While not recording the method used to widen the pass, Thomas Dunn did note that "We were now in the only pass that wagons could possibly get through. About 2 o'clock P.M we found ourselves blockaded by rocks. But after some labor and fatigue we succeeded in getting through."[22] Cooke recorded, "I encountered extraordinary obstacles to a wagon road, and actually hewed a passage, with axes, through a chasm of solid rock, which lacked a foot of being as wide as the wagons. Two of them were taken through in pieces, whilst the work was going on."[23] The labor included lifting wagons and heaving some up on end to maneuver through the narrow gorge. This pass, now known as Box Canyon, is located in California's Anza-Borrego Desert State Park. Several locations within the canyon still bear evidence of where the Mormons had to cut the canyon walls wide enough for their wagons.

Finally, on January 21 circumstances began to change for the better. Thomas Dunn recorded:

> We marched 17 miles to Mr. Warners, an American, the first we had seen since we left Santa Fe. Our road was good this day. We saw more oak timber than we had seen for months before. The soils are much better also. Mr. Warner has on his premises and under his control, 400 Indians, a large stock of cattle and hogs. Sgt. Coray with whom I tented, succeeded in getting 50 lbs. of pork and some flour also. We had been without pork some days. This was quite a rarity.[24]

From Warner's ranch the Battalion began marching toward Los Angeles through deep mud and heavy rains, but on January 25, Cooke received an express from Kearny informing him that Los Angeles had been taken and directing Cooke to meet him in San Diego. Consequently the Battalion changed course and on January 27 reached Mission San Luis Rey, which Samuel Rogers described as "a Catholic church building roofed with tiles, which is the best building I have seen since entering Mexican territory."[25]

That day the Battalion members were awestruck as they caught their first view of the Pacific Ocean. Henry G. Boyle later noted, "I never Shall be able to express my feelings at this enraptured moment. When our colums were halted every eye was turned toward its placid surface, every heart beat with muttered pleasure, evry Soul was full of thankfulness, evry tongue was silen[ce]d, we all felt too ful to give Shape to our feeling by any expression."[26] The sight of the Pacific Ocean caused David Pettigrew to reflect on the experience of their

Early view of San Diego with American flag flying in center, circa 1846. (Courtesy of Bancroft Library, UC Berkeley.)

San Diego
Lith. by E. Weber & Co. Baltro

march: "We shortly came in sight of the Pacific Ocean which to us was a good sight as we had performed a long and tedious march and suffered many hardships and privations both with weariness, hunger, thirst and cold; most of us were barefoot and our clothes were very ragged."[27]

The Battalion soldiers then marched south along El Camino Real, "The King's Highway," to Mission San Diego, arriving January 29. Daniel Tyler described the remarkable difference between the march from San Luis Rey to San Diego and the desert march the Battalion had just completed: "Traveling in sight of the ocean, the clear bright sunshine, with the mildness of the atmosphere, combined to increase the enjoyment of the scene before us. We no longer suffered from the monotonous hardships of the desert and cold atmosphere of the snow-capped mountains. January there, seemed as pleasant as May in the northern States, and the wild oats, grass, mustard and other vegetable growths were as forward as we had been used to seeing them in June. The birds sang sweetly and all nature seemed to smile and join in praise to the Giver of all good."[28]

After arriving in San Diego on January 29, Colonel Philip St. George Cooke penned "Orders No. 1," in which he gave high praise to the accomplishments of the Battalion; his remarks included the oft-quoted line, "History may be searched in vain for an equal march of infantry."[29]

That march took months and covered almost two thousand miles, but the men clearly realized they had accomplished a remarkable feat. While their nearly two-thousand-mile march clearly was not, as some have asserted, the longest military march ever attempted, they had successfully endured unimaginable privation in order to make a viable wagon road between Santa Fe and the Pacific coast, in service to their country. The Mormon Battalion was a volunteer unit; the soldiers had finished their assignment, they missed their families, and the war on the Pacific coast was clearly over, but they still had more than half a year of military service to complete. From January until their discharge in July, most of the Battalion soldiers had to patiently endure the monotonous daily regimen of a soldier's life.

The Mormon Battalion remained at San Diego only a short time before receiving orders to return to San Luis Rey, where they arrived on February 3. On March 14, Company B received orders to return to San Diego, while companies A, C, D, and E marched to Los Angeles. A sick detachment under Lieutenant Oman remained for a time at Mission San Luis Rey.

Unlike the four companies sent to Los Angeles, the soldiers of Company B stationed in San Diego enjoyed a more relaxed and less disciplined service. They were allowed to earn money making bricks, laying brick sidewalks, digging wells, and even constructing a brick courthouse. The citizens of San Diego gratefully acknowledged their services and improvements. Company B remained in San Diego until July 8, when orders were received to march to Los Angeles just prior to their discharge. Some residents of San Diego were so pleased with the Mormon soldiers that a petition was sent to Cooke asking him to station another company of Mormons in their city and that "they did not wish any other soldiers quartered there."[30]

Five days after Company B left for San Diego, companies A, C, D, and E left Mission San Luis Rey for Los Angeles, arriving there on March 23. In contrast to those of Company B, the daily experiences of the soldiers in these companies aligned with standard military duty. In addition to regular drills and guard duty, the soldiers helped build Fort Moore, named after Captain Benjamin D. Moore, who died after being lanced at least a dozen times by Pico's cavalry in the Battle of San Pasqual. Some Battalion soldiers from Los Angeles also guarded the Cajon Pass from Indian attacks. Although the companies stationed in Los Angeles may not have endeared themselves to the local population as the men of Company B had to the citizens of San Diego, their service was equally exemplary and noteworthy. In a letter to Brigadier General Roger Jones written in September 1847, months after the Battalion had been discharged, Colonel Richard B. Mason described the California service and conduct of the Mormon soldiers:

> Of the services of this battalion, of their patience, subordination, and general good conduct, you have already heard; and I take great pleasure in adding, that, as a body of men, they have religiously respected the rights and feelings of these conquered people, and not a syllable of complaint has reached my ears of a single insult offered, or outrage done, by a Mormon volunteer. So high an opinion did I entertain of the battalion, and of their especial fitness for the duties now performed by the garrisons in this country, that I made strenuous efforts to engage their services for another year; but succeeded in engaging but one company, which, as before stated, is now at San Diego. . . . Some few of the discharged Mormons are scattered throughout the country, but the great mass of them have gone to meet their families,

Richard D. Mason (1797–1850) served as military commander of California at the conclusion of the Mexican War. (Courtesy of Bancroft Library, UC Berkeley.)

supposed to be somewhere in the vicinity of Great Salt Lake.[31]

Among many possible reasons, the good conduct of Mormon soldiers may have prompted the order for fifteen of them to return east with General Kearny, who was escorting Colonel John C. Frémont back to Fort Leavenworth for court-martial. At the heart of the matter was Frémont's refusal to obey Kearny's orders. Frémont claimed that Commodore Stockton had appointed him military governor of California, despite the fact that Kearny had received specific authority to govern. Kearny simply was not going to tolerate Frémont's insubordination, and he ordered Frémont to accompany him on the eastbound trip.

The Mormon soldiers who accompanied Kearny left for Monterey in late May and departed Sutter's Fort and set out for Fort Leavenworth by mid-June. After cresting the Sierra Nevada, they came across some of the cannibalized remains of the Donner Party tragedy from the previous winter. Kearny ordered the ghastly body parts collected and buried. After a very rapid two-month journey, they arrived at Fort Leavenworth on August 23. The Mormon escorts soon received their discharge and began traveling north to Council Bluffs, where they arrived during the first two weeks of September, the first Mormon Battalion soldiers to return to their families nearly fourteen months after leaving them camped on the Missouri River. Frémont was tried and found guilty, but the verdict was set aside by President Polk. Still stinging from what he considered an unjust verdict, however, Frémont resigned his commission, a theatrical gesture he would repeat during the Civil War after he was relieved of command after his defeat by "Stonewall" Jackson's forces.

Back in California, as the discharge date approached, the U.S. military commanders began encouraging the Mormon Battalion to reenlist, which created plenty of serious and passionate discussions among the officers and men. Ultimately, each soldier had to decide whether to reenlist or return to the main body of the Church. Now much wiser and more mature, the soldiers debated the benefits and disadvantages of further military service. One fact was certain: on July 16 they would no longer be in the service of the United States Army. For many of them, that date could not come soon enough, as their yearnings to reunite with family grew stronger by the day.

Endnotes

1   Samuel H. Rogers, Reminiscences and Diary, 28 December 1846, Church History Library. Other diarists note the two men visited the camp on December 27. See Thomas J. Dunn, Journal, 27 December 1846, Church History Library.

2   Winston Groom, *Kearny's March: The Epic Creation of the American West, 1846–1847* (New York: Alfred A. Knopf, 2011), 199–212.

3   Levi Hancock, Journal, 5 January 1847, Church History Library.

4   Rogers, Reminiscences and Diary, 28 December 1846, Church History Library.

5   Ibid.

6   Reddick N. Allred, Mormon Battalion experiences and songs, microfilm of typescript, 4, Church History Library.

7   Cooke, *The Conquest of New Mexico and California*, 180.

8   William Coray, Journal, 8 January 1847, quoted in Ricketts, *The Mormon Battalion: U.S. Army of the West*, 110.

9   Rogers, Reminiscences and Diary, 11 January 1847, Church History Library.

10   Tyler, *A Concise History of the Mormon Battalion*, 242–243.

11   Cooke, *The Conquest of New Mexico and California*, 180.

12   Rogers, Reminiscences and Diary, 15 January 1847, Church History Library.

13   William Coray, Journal, Jan. 16, 1847, quoted in Ricketts, *The Mormon Battalion: U.S. Army of the West*, 113.

14   Ibid.; Henry G. Boyle, Reminiscences and Diaries, 16 January 1847, typescript, Church History Library; William Coray, Journal, 16 January 1847, as quoted in Ricketts, *The Mormon Battalion: U.S. Army of the West*, 113.

15   Levi Hancock, Autobiography and Journal [ca. 1878], Church History Library.

16   Cooke, *The Conquest of New Mexico and California*, 185.

17   William Coray, Journal, 16 January 1847, as quoted in Ricketts, *The Mormon Battalion: U.S. Army of the West*, 113.

18   Rogers, Reminiscences and Diary, 16 January 1847, Church History Library.

19   Hancock, Journal, 15 January 1847, Church History Library.

20   Tyler, *A Concise History of the Mormon Battalion*, 244–245.

21   Pettigrew, Journal, 19 January 1847, Church History Library.

22   Dunn, Journal, 18 January 1847, Church History Library.

23   Philip St. George Cooke as quoted in Bigler and Bagley, eds., *Army of Israel*, 182.

24   Dunn, Journal, 18 January 1847, Church History Library.

25   Rogers, Reminiscences and Diary, 27 January 1847, Church History Library.

26   Boyle, Reminiscences and Diaries, 27 January 1847, Church History Library.

27   Pettigrew, Journal, 27 January 1847, Church History Library.

28   Tyler, *A Concise History of the Mormon Battalion*, 253.

29   Philip St. George Cooke, "Orders No. 1," in Tyler, *A Concise History of the Mormon Battalion*, 254–255.

30   Tyler, *A Concise History of the Mormon Battalion*, 289–290.

31   Colonel Richard B. Mason to General Roger Jones, 18 September 1847, in Ex. Doc. No. 17, 31st Congress, 1st Session, in Correspondence relating to the Mormon Battalion, Church History Library. See also Bigler and Bagley, eds., *Army of Israel*.

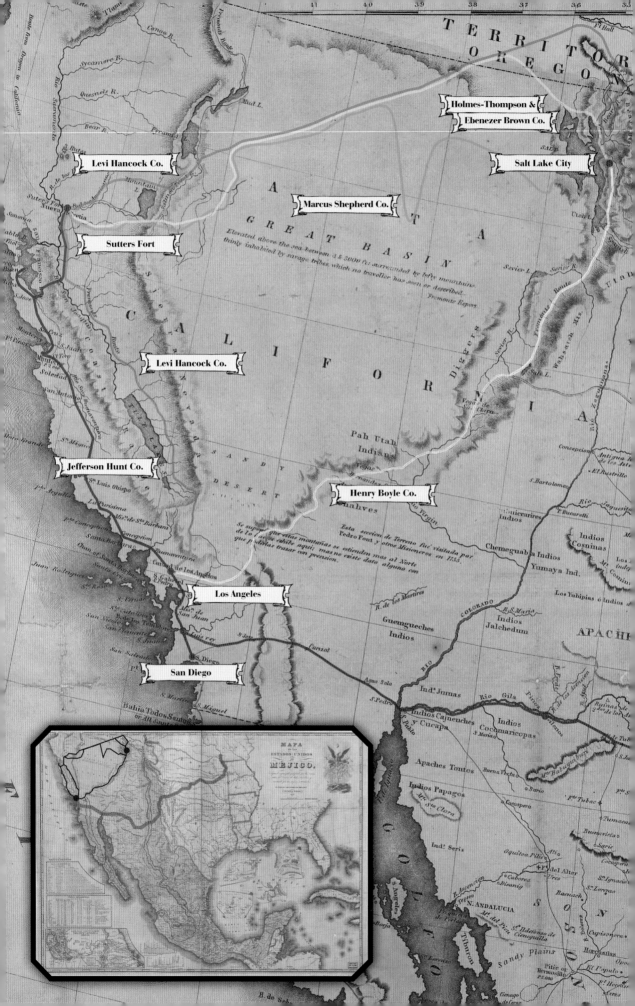

Holmes-Thompson & Ebenezer Brown Co.

Salt Lake City

Levi Hancock Co.

Marcus Shepherd Co.

Sutters Fort

Levi Hancock Co.

Jefferson Hunt Co.

Henry Boyle Co.

Los Angeles

San Diego

Chapter Six

THE IMPACT OF DISCHARGE

"A few days more and we shall go To see our wives & children too"

As the date of their discharge approached, more pressure was brought to bear in an effort to have the men reenlist. After another request for reenlistment was made, Henry Standage wrote, "They cannot in reason expect us to enlist again and especially when they know the treatment we have received . . . hard has been our fare as soldiers."[1] The divisive issue of military versus ecclesiastical authority that had dogged the Mormon Battalion from the time Andrew Jackson Smith took command at Council Grove the previous September resurfaced during the efforts to encourage reenlistment. William Hyde recalled his negative feelings about continuing in military service after Jefferson Hunt and several others had made remarks in favor of reenlisting at a mass meeting of the Battalion soldiers:

> It fell to my lot to be the first to break the silence. I remarked that from the best information which we could gain, the government, in whose service we had been was satisfied with our service, and the Presidency under whose council we had entered service was satisfied, and every feeling of my heart said that all heaven was satisfied, and as for me, let others do as they may, God being my helper, I shall return to my family and to headquarters. I was followed by Father Pettigrew and Brother Daniel Tyler and others, and in their remarks the Spirit of God was manifest, and the eyes of those that wished to see were opened and their situation plainly manifest. And the musical instruments of those that were in favor of reenlisting, were entirely unstrung.[2]

Of course, it was more than just the rigors of army life that caused many to shun reenlistment. Shortly after arriving in San Diego, Robert Stanton Bliss wrote, "My thoughts go to my family continuly how they fare are they well and contented are they looking for the time to meet me in the fall with as much anxiety I do them. Dream of home & its pleasant fireside by, wake only to hear the bugle sound or drums beat for day."[3] Just two weeks before discharge, he penned a poem that included his thoughts about service as well as his hopes for himself, family, and friends:

> A few days more and we shall go
> To see our wives & children too
> And friends so dear we've left below
> To save the Church from overthrow
> Our absence from them has been long
> But oh the time will soon be gone
> When we shall meet once more on earth
> And praise the God that gave us birth.[4]

In addition to distaste for military life and longing for family and friends, timing also factored into the decision of many not to reenlist. Colonel Richard B. Mason described one of the concerns of the men in a letter to Colonel Stevenson, the Southern Military District Commander in Los Angeles:

> I have been informed that one of the objections some of the Mormons express against continuing in service another year is, that it brings to the middle of summer before they are discharged, when it is too late to begin farming; and that if they could be discharged say at the end of March, many would re-enter who otherwise would not.[5]

However, Mason noted that the "law of 13th May last required that the volunteers should enter for twelve months; and, therefore I could not muster them in for a less time but I will pledge that they shall be discharged at the end of March next if they desire it."[6]

Nearly two hundred of the original Mormon Battalion members that enlisted at Council Bluffs never made it to the Pacific coast. At Fort Moore on July 16, 1847, Lieutenant Andrew Jackson Smith, who had so briefly led the Mormon Battalion from Council Grove to Santa Fe, discharged all the Battalion soldiers present in Los Angeles. Absent on that day were the fifteen Battalion soldiers

John C. Frémont (1813–1890), known as the Great Pathfinder, made several exploring expeditions to the West. Kearny charged him with insubordination and he was escorted back to Fort Leavenworth to stand trial. The eastbound escort included fifteen Mormon Battalion soldiers. (Courtesy of the Library of Congress.)

who had been chosen earlier as escorts for General Stephen W. Kearny's trip east for the court-martial of John C. Frémont. The Battalion soldiers who comprised the three sick detachments sent to Pueblo were more than a thousand miles from Los Angeles on July 16. All those in the sick detachments suffered tremendously, and at least nine died while traveling to or wintering in Pueblo. In the spring of 1847, they, along with the "Mississippi Saints," joined Brigham Young and the other Mormons traveling west to the Salt Lake Valley.

Of those discharged in Los Angeles, many felt relieved to conclude their service in the military. However, seventy-nine of the Mormon Battalion soldiers—almost one in four of those who had made the entire march to the Pacific—reenlisted on July 20 for additional service that continued until March 1848. Those who reenlisted became known as the "Mormon Volunteers."

Within days of discharge, almost all of the Mormon Battalion soldiers who did not reenlist organized into companies and began making plans to travel north. Their intended routes would take them either on the El Camino Real, which had connected all the old Spanish missions, or along the western foothills of the Sierra Nevada Mountains. Nearly fifty of the recently discharged men followed Captain Jefferson Hunt along the coast on the El Camino Real as far as Monterey or San Francisco, where a few stayed with Latter-day Saints who had arrived in California in July 1846 under the leadership of Samuel Brannan aboard the ship *Brooklyn*. Captain Hunt, along with others, continued to Sutter's Fort. This was the beginning of a complex story of Battalion veterans traveling various overland routes as they set out to locate and reunite with their families and fellow Church members.

Nearly all of the remaining discharged Mormon soldiers in Los Angeles elected to follow the nominal leadership of Levi Hancock, the acknowledged ecclesiastical leader of the former Battalion. Organized into companies of hundreds, fifties, and tens, the men left about the same time as Hunt's company. Rather than follow the coast route, they opted to travel north from the Los Angeles basin, where they soon crossed Tejón Pass and descended the Tehachapi Mountains into California's Great Central Valley. The brief account by Newman Buckley describes some of the difficulties faced in the early days traveling north from Los Angeles:

Samuel Brannan (1819–1889), pictured here in the upper right with a number of prominent settlers of San Francisco, was leader of the group of Mormons that arrived in Yerba Buena (renamed San Francisco in 1847) aboard the ship *Brooklyn* on July 31, 1846. He later traveled east to meet Brigham Young in an effort to convince Young and the Mormons to continue to the Pacific coast. (Courtesy of Bancroft Library, UC Berkeley.)

My outfit consisted of one Spanish mare, one wild mule, one hundred pounds of flour, a few beans, one pair of pants, two half-worn hickory shirts, the coat with which I left home, one pair of shoes, one blanket, my musket and acoutrements, including some twenty-five rounds of cartridges.

I had not traveled to exceed ten miles, when my pack saddle turned under my mule's belly, and she broke loose from me and ran away. I expected that would be the last I would see of her; but lucky for me, there chanced to be a Spanish boy near by, and I got him to bring her back, for which I paid him the last dollar I had.

I then passed on to Mr. Pecoe's [Pico's] ranch, where my companions made arrangements for forty-four head of wild four-year-old steers, for which we were to pay four dollars per head, with the intention of driving them along for beef. But this proved a failure; we were unable to manage them, and after two days' trial, we were obliged to shoot them all down and jerk the beef. While trying to drive these critters, my riding animal became crippled, and in a few days gave out, and I had to leave her, which left me on foot, to travel and keep up with pack animals, which was very hard to do, as I had to wade or swim all the streams, which, some days, kept me wet from morning till night.[7]

Sutter's Fort in Sacramento as it would have appeared in 1847. (Courtesy of Bancroft Library, UC Berkeley.)

Opposite Top: Early view of Salt Lake City (circa 1858) looking southeast on East Temple Street, later renamed Main Street. A number of discharged veterans of the Mormon Battalion crossed the Sierras and arrived in the Salt Lake Valley in the fall of 1847. (Courtesy of Church History Library.)

Once in the Central Valley, the men traveled north along the foothills of the Sierra Nevada Mountains until they reached Sutter's Fort on the Sacramento River. They arrived at the fort just after Jefferson Hunt and his men had left on August 26 to begin their eastbound trek to the Salt Lake Valley.

Other groups of former Battalion soldiers began leaving Sutter's Fort for Johnson's Ranch on the Bear River (just east of present-day Wheatland, California) during the last week of August, where they reassembled and began their eastward march to the Salt Lake Valley on the Truckee route of the California Trail. Not subject to military discipline, they kept their own pace, and soon the companies were traveling about two days apart. On September 6, they encountered Samuel Brannan returning from an unsuccessful attempt to persuade Brigham Young to locate the Saints on the Pacific coast; a day later, they ran in to James Brown, who was traveling to collect the Battalion payroll at Brigham Young's request. Brown brought with him a letter to Jefferson Hunt along with verbal instructions from Brigham Young that explained that he wanted only those with sufficient means to come to the Salt Lake Valley; because provisions were so scarce, he wanted the others to remain in California. Consequently, about half of the company returned to the Sacramento Valley while the rest continued traveling to the Salt Lake Valley.

Among those who proceeded to the Salt Lake Valley was Jefferson Hunt. After staying in the valley just one month, he—accompanied by Orrin Porter Rockwell, Asahel A. Lathrop, Elijah Knapp Fuller, and fifteen other packers—headed south on November 16, hoping to obtain seeds, fruit tree cuttings, and possibly milk cows in Los Angeles. Near present-day Parowan, Utah, they intersected the Spanish Trail and followed it into the Los Angeles basin, arriving in early January 1848. Rockwell stayed behind, and three Indians joined the group; on February 15, the small pack train set out again for the Salt Lake Valley, arriving about May 10. In less than a year, Jefferson Hunt had traveled north from Los Angeles to Sutter's Fort on the Sacramento; left Sutter's Fort eastbound over the Sierra Nevada; crossed what is today Nevada and western Utah to the Salt Lake Valley; traveled south to the Spanish Trail and followed it to Los Angeles; and then returned via the Spanish Trail to present-day southern Utah, where he turned north to the Salt Lake Valley. Hunt's remarkable travel between July 1847 and May 1848 is but one example of the fact that the Mormon Battalion march instilled confidence in many former soldiers in traveling great distances, often across unfamiliar terrain. Like Hunt, other former Battalion soldiers arrived in the Great Salt Lake Valley in mid-October 1847. Some discovered to their dismay that their families were still in Iowa and made immediate plans to travel east to Council Bluffs. William Pace, one of those who intended to continue traveling

William B. Pace (1832–1907) was only fourteen years old when he was hired to travel with the Mormon Battalion as a servant to his father, First Lieutenant James Pace of Company E. After discharge, the Paces traveled to Winter Quarters to locate their family. (Courtesy of Church History Library.)

Upon reaching Salt Lake City in the fall of 1847, a number of Battalion veterans proceeded east another one thousand miles to Winter Quarters to reunite with their families. This scene by C. C. A. Christensen depicts Winter Quarters, which served as the transitory settlement along the Missouri River for thousands of Latter-day Saints from 1846–1848. (Courtesy of Church History Museum.)

east, recalled the stopover in the Salt Lake Valley: "Provisions being scarce in the valley, we were told we could get supplies at Fort Bridger and at Laramie reasonable, and it would be a great help to the people if we would leave our provisions and replenish on the road. Having a common interest we unloaded our supplies, taking only what was supposed enough to do us to Fort Bridger."[8] Along with Pace, at least thirty-one others soon left the Salt Lake Valley headed east. Enduring brutally harsh winter conditions, the men traveled a thousand miles, arriving at the Winter Quarters-Council Bluffs area on December 18. One of them, William Hyde, left an account of the difficult circumstances that the men faced on December 9, 1847, and how Providence favored them the following day:

> On the 9th we camped within about 15 miles of the [Elk]horn [River], which place is 30 miles from the general camp of the Saints, or Winter Quarters. But as we were strangers to the route, we were not aware that we were so near our place of destination, and as the snow was deep, and our meat which we had saved from the horse entirely exhausted, we seated ourselves upon the snow around our camp fire and entered into council as to the wisest course to be pursued. Some thought best to send two men on two of the best mules in camp for Winter Quarters. To this I replied that

we had now traveled near five thousand miles, and that we had suffered much with hunger, cold, thirst and fatigue, and now to give out on the last hundred miles I didn't like the idea. I then said that in case we could not get through with out, we would make a free will offering of my riding mule and we would eat her, as she was in as good order as any in camp. To this proposition all readily agreed.

On the morning of the 10th, we were all united in calling on the Lord to regard our situation in mercy and send us food from an unexpected quarter that we might have wherewith to subsist upon. And here the Lord heard our prayer. Soon after reaching the [Elk]Horn [River], the wild turkeys began to pass our camp in droves, and such a sight I never before witnessed. Drove after drove continued to pass through the woods until night set in. We succeeded in getting four, which was one to every four persons, and after this we could not get any more although our shots might be considered ever so fair, and we concluded to be satisfied. Probably it would have been a damage to us if we had got all we wanted as we were then suffering in the extreme with hunger.[9]

Hyde and his companions made it to the Winter Quarters-Council Bluffs area seven days later.

After receiving Brigham Young's instructions not to proceed to the Salt Lake Valley, many of those who returned to the Sacramento Valley worked in one of John Sutter's enterprises. Six of them—William Barger, Henry Bigler, James S. Brown, William Johnstun, Azariah Smith, and Alexander Stephens—were employed by Sutter's partner, James Marshall, to construct a sawmill at Coloma on the south fork of the American River. On January 24, 1848, Marshall discovered gold in the mill's tailrace. The date and the discoverer are known because Bigler and Smith noted the event in their journals.

James W. Marshall (1810–1885) discovered gold on the south fork of the American River on January 24, 1848, setting off the historic California Gold Rush. (Courtesy of Bancroft Library, UC Berkeley.)

James Wilson Marshall
discoverer of gold in California

Houseworth,   Photographer.

Bigler recorded, "Monday 24th this day some kind of mettle was found in the tail race that looks like goald," later inserting, "first discovered by James Martial [Marshall], the Boss of the Mill." The following week, Bigler noted: "Our metal has been tride and proves to be goald it is thought to be rich. We have pict up more than a hundred dollars worth last week."[10] Although written a few days after the event, Azariah Smith noted, "This week Mon the 24th, Mr Marshall found some pieces of (as we all suppose) gold, and he has gone to the Fort for the purpose of finding out. It is found in the raceway in small pieces, some have been found that would weigh five dollars." On February 20, 1848, he wrote, "Today I picked up a little more of the root of all evil."[11]

The discovery sparked the historic California Gold Rush. Henry Bigler soon had gold fever, and his diary reflected his gold-hunting adventures:

Portrait of four of the six Mormon Battalion veterans (l to r: Henry W. Bigler, Azariah Smith, William J. Johnstun, and James S. Brown) who helped construct Sutter's Mill roughly 40 miles northeast of Sutter's Fort. This image was taken in January 1898 at the fiftieth anniversary of the discovery of gold. (Courtesy of Church History Library.)

On Sunday, February 6th, [1848] Barger and I went over the river opposite the saw-mill to look for gold. I found six dollars' worth and Barger about two-thirds as much.

Six days later I borrowed Brown's gun and went down the river to hunt ducks, as was supposed, but in reality to prospect for gold. When about a half mile below the mill I saw on the opposite side of the river bare rocks of the same kind as were in the tail race, looking as though there had been a land slide, leaving the base rock to view. It struck me so forcibly that there might be gold, I pulled off my clothing and waded over, and sure enough I found it, and picked up to the amount of one dollar and fifty cents . . .

On February 22nd the ground was white with snow, which prevented our working at the mill. I therefore set out to hunt for deer, but soon changed my mind and went to my mine. I waded the river as usual, after removing every stitch of my clothing. The river was rising and the water was almost as cold as ice itself. It was also deep and swift, and I was scarcely able to walk. When I got over my feet were very cold. I tried to strike fire, but my hands were so benumbed with cold I could not hold my flint and steel. I tried to catch fire from my gun but [it] being wet I could not fire it, and at last I was forced to dance, jump and run over the rocks until I got warmed up and went to work, having nothing but my pocket knife to work with. Since the morning the weather had moderated and a heavy, misty rain had set in, causing the snow to soon disappear. I searched closely every crevice and finally went down near the water's edge in the sand, where I began to find it more plentifully though in very fine particles, except one piece of pure gold nearly round like a bullet, worth between five and six dollars. I almost felt I had found a fortune on picking it out of the sand . . . On reaching the shanty the boys began to quiz me and wanted to know what luck, where my game was, why out so late, and why I did not cross the dam that morning, etc. They had suspected at last. I called for the scales and found twenty-two and a half dollars' worth of clean gold as the result of my day's hunt. The secret now being out I told them, of course, all about my discovery.

The mill hands came very near deserting their employer and turning their attention to hunting gold, but on second consideration thought it a pity to leave before the mill was finished.[12]

Located on the south fork of the American River in Coloma, Sutter's Mill was the site of James W. Marshall's gold discovery. Six recently discharged Mormon Battalion veterans were employed at the sawmill and two of their diaries documented the event. (Courtesy of Bancroft Library, UC Berkeley.)

Nathan Hawk described the early methods the former soldiers employed to find gold:

I told you awhile ago that I mined a few days at Mormon Island, and it was the "dust" that I took out of there that I carried East with me. Well, it was mining in a primitive way. We had no pans, no lumber to make rockers, and so we used Indian baskets to pan with. The Indians made a watertight willow basket that answered the place of a pan. When we would get panned down to the black sand we would dump the gold on a flour sack which we had spread out upon the grass.

In order to weigh our gold, we made a balance with two chips, a stick and a string. We imitated the scales held by Jus[t]ice. We placed the gold on one chip and [a] Mexican or Spanish gold coin on the other until they balanced; in that way we could pretty closely estimate the value of our day's work, which averaged about $20 to the man.[13]

As the summer of 1848 approached, many of the Mormon Battalion veterans faced the decision of whether to remain in California and capitalize on the gold discovery or leave the prospect of riches and travel to the Salt Lake Valley to rejoin the main body of the Church and their families. James S. Brown later recorded:

The day before starting from the gold diggings was a kind of an off-day, in which [I] . . . wandered off from camp, with pick and shovel, up a dry gulch where [I] soon struck a very rich prospect of gold . . . By sundown had washed out forty-nine dollars and fifty cents in gold; yet . . . strange as it may appear . . . I have never seen that rich spot of earth since; nor do I regret it, for there always has been a higher object before me than gold. We had covenanted to move together . . . We were in honor bound to move the next day. We did move, leaving that rich prospect without ever sticking a stake in the gulch, but abandoning it to those who might follow . . . People said, "Here is gold on the bedrock, gold on the hills, gold in the rills, gold everywhere, gold to spend, gold to lend, gold for all that will delve, and soon you can make an independent fortune." We could realize all that. Still duty called, our honor was at stake, we had covenanted with each other, there was a principle involved; for with us it was God and His kingdom first. We had friends and relatives in the wilderness, yea, in an untried, desert land, and who knew their condition? We did not. So it was duty before pleasure, before wealth, and with this prompting we rolled out and joined our comrades.[14]

Brown's statement, made retrospectively, needs some qualification. Before departing for the Salt Lake Valley, at least some of

James S. Brown (1828–1902) was a member of the Holmes-Thompson Company of Mormon Battalion veterans who crossed the Sierras in the summer of 1848. (Courtesy of Church History Library.)

the former Mormon Battalion soldiers apparently had made significant amounts of money. John Sutter recorded, "Paid off all the Mormons which have been employed by me in building these mills and other mechanical trades, all of them made their pile and some of them became very rich and wealthy but all of them are bound to the Great Salt Lake and [will] spend their fortunes there to the glory and honor of the Lord."[15]

In the summer of 1848, many former Mormon Battalion members, including Brown and some of the Saints who had arrived in California on the ship *Brooklyn*, met in the Sierra Nevada foothills at a place they named Pleasant Valley. They began blazing a new trail east over the Sierra Nevada, leaving behind the newly discovered goldfields. The first company to leave—forty-five men along with William Coray's wife, Melissa—began the eastward journey under the leadership of former Battalion members Jonathan Holmes and Samuel Thompson. Due to the difficulty in taking wagons over Donner Pass and along the Truckee River, they hoped to blaze an easier route through the mountains somewhere near the head of the American River. James S. Brown described both their reasoning and their confidence: "As we had become accustomed to pioneer life it was thought we could find a better route."[16] Ezra H. Allen, Daniel Browett, and Henderson Cox left on June 25 and traveled ahead of the company to determine the best route.

When the three scouts failed to return, everyone in the Holmes-Thompson company—which began its trek over the Sierra Nevada a week later—became uneasy. Tragically, the bodies of the three men were found in a shallow grave not far from the summit of Carson Pass. The company named the site Tragedy Spring. As Henry Bigler described it, the three men were "supposed to have been murdered and buried by Indians."[17] The company reinterred the three victims, placed a rock wall around the graves, and inscribed a memorial tribute into a nearby tree. Samuel H. Rogers recorded:

> We found to our regreat and deep sorrow of
> heart the Bodies of the Three Brethren, who went
> in search of the road viz Daniel Browatt [Browett],
> Henderson Cocks [Cox] and Ezra H Allen. By
> the appearance and signs we could discover, they
> ware taken by supprise, when they ware asleep
> in the night. Arrows ware found round about.
> Allen['s]. . . purce was found which he forme[r]ly
> carried suspendid from his neck. The string was
> cut in two. Blood was on the purce. Gold dust
> and coin money was in it. The time they had been
> absent from us was twenty four days. They are sup-
> posed to have been Murdered on the 27 of June in

the night. We kept a gard to protect us from the Indians.[18]

Jonathan Holmes gave additional details in his account of the tragedy:

> [July 19, 1848] Found whear those 3 Brethren ware Murdered Namely Daniel Brewett Ezra H. Allen & Henderson Cox. . . . We fixed the grave as well as we could it was a Solem time when it was asertained that these men had been murderd & in so shocking a maner it was a time of Solemnity & morning to think that the man that was to Be our leader to Salt Lake was now lying Dead, he was like a father to me & we morn his loss.

> [July 20, 1848] Staid in Camp & fixt our wagon & Built a wall round the Graves of our Brethren that had Ben Murdered &t&t.[19]

Henry Bigler noted the text carved into the tree to mark the tragedy:

> We cut the following inscription on a Balsome fir that stood near the grave. "To the memory of Daniel Browett and Ezrah H. Allen, Henderson Cox who was supposed to have been murdered and buried by Indians on the night of the 27th of June, A.D. 1848.["] We called this place tragedy Spring.[20]

Ezra Allen's widow, Sarah, later described the agony she experienced on learning of her husband's murder as well as her faith that helped her cope with the loss:

> In the spring of 1848, I began to look forward to the return of my husband. The Lord had blessed my efforts to provide for my family. And the Brethren and Sisters had been kind to me. But a long journey lay before me and I looked forward to the time when his strong arms would lift these burdens of care from my shoulders. I gathered grapes

from the lowland near the river and made wine and prepared such dainties as I could that would please him. At length the news came that a company of brethren was expected to cross the river in a few days. I felt anxious to go to the ferry to meet him, but circumstances would not permit, so I remained at home waiting and watching, listening to the sound of every footstep that approached my door. After several days word was brought to me that some of the brethren had arrived home and that my husband and two other of the brethren had been killed by Indians in the California Mountains. . . . I learned that a purse containing $120.00 in gold dust had been found belonging to my husband and it was being brought to me. Thus, when my hopes and expectations [were] blasted in a moment, what could I do but trust in God. I had no relative in the Church, two small children and a journey of 1000 miles before me. For some time I felt I would sink under my burden of grief and anguish of heart. Then I aroused myself and began to meditate on what course to pursue, how to provide for my family and prepare for the journey. I therefore determined to make every effort in my power to accomplish this desirable undertaking and leave the event in the hands of God. In a few days, the purse . . . which had belonged to my husband was brought to me. There were marks of blood upon it and it seemed to me as the price of his life.[21]

The tragic site was almost always mentioned in the diaries of westbound emigrants traveling the Carson Trail to the goldfields. Often the words cut into the tree were included in the diary entries. After winter storms damaged the tree in the late 1920s, the portion of the tree bearing the inscription was removed and placed at Sutter's Fort State Historic Park in August 1931. The California Department of Parks and Recreation later moved it to the Marshall Gold Discovery State Historic Park at Coloma.

Traveling with much more caution, the company left Tragedy Spring, crested the 9,500-foot West Pass and the 8,500 foot Carson Pass, and began the difficult descent along the west fork of the Carson River. The company reached the Carson Valley on August 4, 1848, and continued following the Carson River for a week until they reached the main California Trail. Behind them came other groups of former Mormon Battalion soldiers, also on their way to Salt Lake. After crossing the waterless forty-mile stretch of the Carson Sink, they came to and began following the Humboldt River in what is today north-central Nevada. The eastbound Holmes-Thompson Company soon encountered mountaineer Samuel J. Hensley and his westbound company of packers. Hensley's pack train had come from the Salt Lake Valley. Henry Bigler recorded the first description of the Salt Lake Cutoff after the Holmes-Thompson Company visited with Hensley:

> We was met by Capt. S. Hinsley [and] a packing company of 10 men. we got a way bill of our Road from here to salt lake and not [to] go by Ft. Hall and save a bout 8 or 10 days travel. we learn from Mr. Hinsley that it is not more than a bout 380 miles to the lake [and] to take a serten cut off which we are sure to find with plenty of wood and water and grass [by] a route that he cum but waggons have never went there before. a good waggon rout.[22]

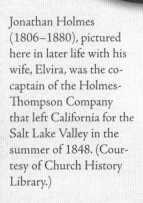

Jonathan Holmes (1806–1880), pictured here in later life with his wife, Elvira, was the co-captain of the Holmes-Thompson Company that left California for the Salt Lake Valley in the summer of 1848. (Courtesy of Church History Library.)

Following the Holmes-Thompson Company along the same route was the Ebenezer Brown Company, composed of Battalion veterans and Saints from the ship *Brooklyn*. Some, like company captain Ebenezer Brown, had been among the seventy-nine Mormon Volunteers who had reenlisted after their discharge from the Mormon Battalion. Two pack companies composed of Battalion veterans also traveled east from California to the Salt Lake Valley in the summer and fall of 1848.

The composition of the third and final 1848 pack company to leave present-day northern California for the Salt Lake Valley is not known, but it was captained by Marcus Sheperd, the only known Battalion veteran in the group. His pack train left California in October and took the Hastings Cutoff to the Salt Lake Valley.

Regarding the Spanish Trail from present-day southern California, no one had ever attempted to bring wagons on this route. However, after the Mormon Volunteers completed their additional eight months of military service, a company with thirty-five members under the leadership of Henry G. Boyle and guided by Porter Rockwell left the Los Angeles area on April 12 and arrived in the Salt Lake Valley on June 5, about a month after Hunt's pack train. Boyle's company included a wagon, and their journey proved that wagon travel was feasible on the route from the Salt Lake Valley to the Spanish Trail and on to southern California.[23] That fact would become important during the California Gold Rush of 1849.

Hensley's Salt Lake Cutoff and the route from the Spanish Trail to the Salt Lake Valley, established as viable wagon routes by discharged Mormon Battalion veterans, became important transportation routes for some of the thousands of westbound Argonauts headed for the California goldfields in 1849. At the request of Brigham Young and other Church leaders, some Mormon Battalion veterans returned to California in 1849 on what can loosely be termed "gold missions." Some of these ex-soldiers turned missionaries would mine for gold in an effort to provide for elderly individuals in the Salt Lake Valley, while others mined gold to finance their passage to a missionary field of labor, including places as far away as Hawaii and Tahiti. All of these incidental events involving former Battalion soldiers—discovering gold, blazing transportation routes, funding missions—would not have occurred without their enlistment as volunteers and their participation in the march of the Mormon Battalion. More importantly, it was not just a matter of coincidental timing. The seasoned maturity gained during their months of military service prepared them to successfully accomplish each new challenge they encountered. That pattern would repeat itself throughout their lives as they served their families and the Church as colonizers, public servants, missionaries, and Church leaders for most of the remaining decades of the nineteenth century.

Endnotes

1   Standage, Journal, 18 June 1847, in Golder, ed., *The March of the Mormon Battalion*, 221.

2   Hyde, 29 June 1847, Church History Library.

3   Bliss, Diary, 15 February 1847, Church History Library.

4   Ibid., 4 July 1847.

5   Colonel Richard B. Mason to Colonel J. D. Stevenson, 5 June 1847, in Ex. Doc. No. 17, 31st Congress, 1st-Session, in Correspondence relating to the Mormon Battalion, Church History Library.

6   Ibid.

7   Newman Bulkley, "Fifteen Months' Experience," *Juvenile Instructor* 17, no. 21 (1 Nov. 1882): 334.

8   William Byram Pace, Autobiography, 1904, 8, Church History Library.

9   Hyde, 9–10 December 1847, Church History Library; Hyde, *The Private Journal of William Hyde*, 48.

10 Henry W. Bigler, Diary, 24 January 1848, Society of California Pioneers, San Francisco, California.

11 David L. Bigler, ed., *The Gold Discovery Journal of Azariah Smith* (Salt Lake City: University of Utah Press, 1990), 110.

12 [Henry W. Bigler] Henele Pikale, "Recollections of the Past," *Juvenile Instructor* 21 (15 December 1886), as quoted in Kenneth N. Owens, *Gold Rush Saints: California Mormons and the Great Rush for Riches*, Kingdom in the West: The Mormons and the American Frontier Series, vol. 7 (Spokane, WA: The Arthur H. Clark Company, 2004), 115–116.

13 Nathan Hawk, Interview, *The [Sacramento] Evening Bee*, 4 January 1906, as quoted in Owens, *Gold Rush Saints*, 127.

14 Brown, *Life of a Pioneer*, 15, 119–120.

15 John A. Sutter, et al., *New Helvetia Diary: A Record of Events Kept by John A. Sutter and His Clerks at New Helvetia, California, from September 9, 1815 to May 25, 1848* (San Francisco, CA: Grabhorn Press, 1939), 129–135, as quoted in Owens, *Gold Rush Saints*, 160–161.

16 Brown, *Life of a Pioneer*, 110.

17 Henry W. Bigler, Daybook, 20 July 1848, Bancroft Library, University of California, Berkeley, as quoted in Owens, *Gold Rush Saints*, 172–173.

18 Rogers, Reminiscences and Diary, 19 July 1848, Church History Library.

19 Jonathan H. Holmes, Diary, 19–20 July 1848, Church History Library.

20 Bigler, Daybook, 20 July 1848, as quoted in Owens, *Gold Rush Saints*, 172–173.

21 Sarah Fiske Allen, Reminiscences, in Preston Nibley, "A Bag of Gold Dust," *Church News*, 28 June 1941, 8; Sarah Beriah Fiske Allen Ricks, A Brief Sketch of the Life of Sarah Beriah Fiske Allen Ricks, 12, Pioneer History Collection, Daughters of Utah Pioneers Museum, Salt Lake City, Utah.

22 Henry Bigler, Reminiscences and Diaries, 1846–1850, volume 2, 1–13, Church History Library.

23 Journal History, 5 June 1848, Church History Library.

A NEW MAP OF THE
STATE OF
CALIFORNIA
THE TERRITORIES OF
OREGON, WASHINGTON
UTAH &
NEW MEXICO

SCALE OF MILES.

PUBLISHED BY CHARLES DESILVER
No 251 Market Street Philadelphia

EXPLANATION.
Capitals of Territories .... *
Cities, Towns & Villages .... •
Military & Trading Posts .... +
Routes of Pacific Railroad ....

EPILOGUE

On February 2, 1848, six months after the Mormon Battalion was discharged from military service, the Treaty of Guadalupe Hidalgo was signed, ending the Mexican War and ceding more than a half million square miles of Mexican territory to the United States.

While the members of the Mormon Battalion figured in that war, they never engaged Mexican forces in combat. Instead, the role of the Battalion soldiers was defined by marching, not fighting, and centered on opening a practical wagon route to the Pacific coast. The route the Battalion soldiers established, known as Cooke's Wagon Road, became a major emigration and freighting route and led to the 1853 Gadsden Purchase, a thirty-thousand-square-mile land acquisition from Mexico in present-day southern Arizona.

After discharge from the military, many former Battalion soldiers were witnesses to and participants in the great California Gold Rush. But believing Church and family were more important than gold, most of them left California. In their return home, they blazed the Carson route, also known as the Mormon-Carson Emigrant Trail, a wagon road that became the preferred route to Gold-Rush California in 1849 and 1850. Some of these former soldiers also established Hensley's Salt Lake Cutoff as a viable wagon route from the Salt Lake Valley to the main California Trail in present-day southern Idaho. There was an additional benefit to their service: A portion of the Mormon Battalion pay and clothing allowance helped the Church when it was in very financially trying circumstances and was a significant factor in helping finance Mormon emigration to the Great Basin.

In 1846, at a time when the Church faced some of its most severe trials and when many Church members were struggling just to survive, Brigham Young's bold decision to encourage—even solicit—the recruitment of five hundred men to serve as a battalion in the Mexican War must have been difficult to understand. Yet his request was fulfilled through the faith of those who enlisted and served and

This 1857 map shows the Gadsden Purchase in current-day southern Arizona and New Mexico. Purchased from Mexico by the United States in 1853 for $10 million, this thirty-thousand-square-mile region is one of the lasting impacts of the march of the Mormon Battalion. (Courtesy of David Rumsey Map Collection, Stanford University.)

by the faith of the families who were left behind. The service and accomplishments of the Mormon Battalion are still remembered and honored by the Church and by descendants. Various locations commemorate their service and accomplishments, including the Mormon Battalion monument located on the grounds of the Utah State Capitol as well as the recently remodeled Mormon Battalion Historic Site in Old Town San Diego.

It is interesting that the story of the Mormon Battalion looms so large in Mormon culture and yet barely merits a footnote in scholarly works about the Mexican War. Historian Sherman Fleek has insightfully noted that the "fact that it [the Battalion] did not fight is perhaps the most obvious reason; perhaps the difficulty of dealing with the complex culture, theology, and related dimensions of the Mormon faith has discouraged a serious military study."[1] Whether the arduous march of the Battalion was of any consequence in the outcome of the Mexican War is of little importance to many descendants of those who served. The larger context of why the Mormon Battalion existed at all is not even considered in some family-produced biographical works of Battalion soldiers. Often such authors briefly note an ancestor's participation in the march, followed by a much more lengthy description of the ancestor's post-Battalion life. In many of these hagiographies, the Battalion ancestor becomes an iconic figure, masking the complexity of his real character and personality.

The Battalion soldier as icon is more than mere ancestor veneration. For many, the Mormon Battalion is a symbolic representation of principles—such as sacrifice, obedience, and devotion to family and church—that are highly valued in Mormon culture. Likewise, Mormon pioneers who "crossed the plains" are viewed as epitomizing these same principles. The symbolic importance of these two groups perhaps explains why those in the Mormon Battalion are more often viewed as "pioneers" rather than soldiers. Yet the linkage of pioneer and soldier is based on more than just a symbolic representation of values. The experience, maturity, and self-confidence gained by the soldiers of the Mormon Battalion during their remarkable march enabled them to assume a wide range of postmilitary roles, including the role of pioneer.

The reservoir of experienced men that came out of the Mormon Battalion proved a blessing to the Church in countless settings throughout the balance of the nineteenth century. The postmilitary experiences of a few Battalion soldiers cited in this volume evidence the lasting value of their yearlong service. It has already been noted that after his discharge from the Battalion, Henry Bigler was deeply connected to the events that led to the California Gold Rush. After arriving in the Salt Lake Valley in the fall of 1848, his stay was relatively short. In October 1849, just one year later, he headed back to California with a few others at the request of Brigham Young as a "gold missionary." It was not an assignment he readily embraced:

> This intelligence was unexpectedly received by me. I was not looking for any such mission. Indeed it had been the Presidents counsil not to go to the gold mines. . . When word came to me that Father Smith wished me to go I hesitated, however as he had sent for me I went and seen him when he explained to me what the President had said and the counsil President Young had given to him in relation to sending a man to the mines etc. After I had consented to go I could not help feeling sorrowful and a reluctance to go for I feel attached to this place and to this people for they are my brethren and dear friends and it was with some strugle with my feelings that I consented to go.[2]

After a difficult trip to southern California and after traveling up the coast, across the San Joaquin Valley to the Mariposa mines, and then north to the American River, Bigler and his companions engaged in the difficult work of mining gold. In late September 1850, Bigler recorded a visit from apostle Charles C. Rich:

> This morning the brethren was called together at our tent by Bro. Rich. he stated he wanted some of us to go on a mission to the Sandwich Islands to preach the gospel that his opinion was it would cost us no more to spend the winter thare than it would here, that we could make nothing in the wintertime in consequence of so much water in the streams, and another thing provisions would be higher in the mines and it would cost us more to stay here amd make nothing than it would if we went to the islands and preach. in his opinion it would be the best thing we could do and the best council he could give. it would be like killing 2 birds with one stone for we would live thare as cheap and perform a mission at the same time. he then called upon ten of us. . . he then laid his hands on us and sat us apart for the above mission, and blest us in the name of the Lord, and told us to act as the spirit dictated after we got there. in a fiew minutes he took his leave leaveing his peace and blessing with us. we felt well though sorrow[ful]

Henry W. Bigler (1815–1900) was a member of Company B, served multiple missions to Hawaii, and spent the last years of his life working in the St. George Temple at the request of Brigham Young. (Courtesy of Church History Library.)

to have him leave so soon. I have been at work ever since my arrival in the mines which was the last of February exposeing mysef, liveing out in rains & snows, traveling and prospecting building and repaireing dams working up to my neck in water, and for weeks in water up to my wast & arms and have made but little, the expenses over run the gain. in August I sent $100 to Father Smith by Bro. A. Lyman. we expect to finish our claim in a fiew days and then leave for our field of labour.[3]

Henry Bigler would spend much of the next four years as a missionary in Hawaii before returning to the Salt Lake Valley. After returning from Hawaii to Utah Territory, he married, began to raise a family, and within just three years he was called to serve another mission to Hawaii. He departed for his mission in May 1857 expecting to be gone from home and family possibly for years. But when it was learned that the U.S. Army was headed for Utah Territory to end a supposed Mormon sedition in a conflict known as the Utah War, Bigler and other missionaries serving in Hawaii, as well as several hundred others serving throughout the world, were directed to return home and defend Zion.

Like Bigler, James S. Brown, who "had become accustomed to pioneer life" and who felt he and his former Battalion friends could "find a better route," left California and helped blaze a new route to the Salt Lake Valley in the fall of 1848.[4] With Bigler and others, he returned to California in 1849 and was called to serve a mission to Tahiti in 1850. After returning to Utah Territory, he served two more missions: one to the Indians, and another to England from 1860 to 1862. In March 1888, he was briefly imprisoned for unlawful cohabitation. From 1892 to 1893 he served yet another mission in Tahiti. He served as patriarch of the Salt Lake Stake in the later years of his life and died in March 1903. Brown's funeral was held in the Assembly Hall on Temple Square in Salt Lake City. The speakers included Church President Joseph F. Smith, Apostle Brigham Young Jr. and Salt Lake Stake President Angus M. Cannon, who stated that James S. Brown "has been true and faithful as a soldier and missionary, and his friends on the other side will welcome him in their hearts."[5]

Because of his extensive postdischarge travels in 1847 and 1848, former Battalion member Jefferson Hunt was considered qualified to guide a large wagon train composed primarily of gold-seeking emigrants on their way to California who had arrived in the Salt Lake Valley too late to cross the Sierra Nevada. The company, which traveled from the Salt Lake Valley to southern California, included fellow Battalion veterans Henry Bigler and James S. Brown, along with other "gold missionaries." After returning to the Salt Lake Valley in 1850, Hunt once again traveled to California with more than four hundred colonists to establish the Mormon colony of San Bernardino in 1851. He held the rank of brigadier general in the California militia and served four terms in the California legislature, becoming the second most senior member of the lower house. Because of the Utah War, Hunt heeded the call to return to Utah Territory in 1857. For many years he lived in the Utah town of Huntsville, which was named after him, before moving to Oxford, Idaho, where he died in 1879.

Henry Standage (1818–1899) was a member of Company E. Following his military service, Standage colonized numerous communities in Utah and Arizona. (Courtesy of International Society Daughters of Utah Pioneers, Salt Lake City.)

Henry Standage arrived in the Salt Lake Valley in 1847 and remained there until 1851. Between 1852 and 1856 he lived in or helped colonize Provo, Fillmore, Bingham Fort (now Ogden), and, finally, Brigham City. In 1860 Standage uprooted his family to accept an assignment to establish the town of Richmond in Cache Valley. For eighteen of the twenty years he resided in Richmond he served as postmaster. He also served for many years as justice of the peace and managed the Church's cooperative store. In 1880, he moved his family to Arizona, originally intending to locate on the San Pedro River, the very river he traveled along as a member of the Battalion thirty-four years earlier. However, Standage opted to return to the Salt River Valley and settled in the Mormon community of Mesa, where he lived until his death in 1899.

After arriving in the Salt Lake Valley, Henry G. Boyle remained there until 1851, when he, like Jefferson Hunt, traveled in the company led by Amasa Lyman and Charles C. Rich to southern California, where he helped establish San Bernardino. In 1855 Lyman and Rich sent him on a mission to northern California in an effort to collect funds to help pay off the mortgage on the San Bernardino ranch. In April 1856, Boyle was again called on a mission to northern California and served under the direction of George Q. Cannon until October 1857. During that time he baptized more than fifty people and helped establish branches of the Church in Yolo and Sonoma counties. As a result of the Utah War, he left southern California for Utah Territory, arriving in February 1858. The following April, under the direction of Amasa Lyman, Boyle was part of an exploring party to the Colorado River and the Mojave Indians. After returning, he first made his home in Salt Lake City, before moving to Payson, where he taught school.

In 1867 Boyle was called to serve the first of seven missions to the southern states, where he eventually served as the first president of the Southern States Mission from 1876–1878. During the short intervals between these missions he taught school.

In 1878, he was also elected chaplain of the Utah Territorial Legislature, and following another mission to the southern states, he opened a business in Payson in "connection with the firm of Higginbotham & Brother," noting that he felt he "could do a good business at Payson, selling Merchandise and buying all kinds of grain vegetables fruits butter Eggs etc."[6]

In October 1887, Boyle was arrested, convicted, and imprisoned in the Utah Territorial Penitentiary for unlawful cohabitation. Writing from prison, he reflected on the values in life that for him mattered most:

Henry G. Boyle (1824–1902) was a member of Company C. After discharge, he reenlisted as one of the Mormon Volunteers and led a group on the western leg of the Old Spanish Trail and blazed a new route to the Salt Lake Valley. (Courtesy of Church History Library.)

> I think that in order to learn the great lesson of life, thoroughly, we should have to contend to some extent with poverty. Therefore I can acknowledge the hand of the Lord in poverty. And although we are deprived of many of the good things that wealth enables us to procure in this life, I trust we may be able to lay a sure foundation for an inheritance of wealth in that life to come, that will be enduring as Eternity, and will not fade away. And for the enjoyment of which we should be fully prepared by past experience.[7]

Boyle added, "I see my life of service as something that will endure eternally." [8] Boyle eventually moved to Arizona, where he died in 1908. His military experience helped prepare him, like so many of his Battalion companions, for that life of service.

Bigler, Brown, Hunt, Standage, and Boyle—indeed, all the soldiers of the Mormon Battalion—while in active U.S. military service provided, as Brigham Young expressed it, "the temporal salvation of our camp . . . and it has proved a weapon of our defense, a blockade in the way of our worst enemies under which the widows, the poor and the destitute, and in fact all of this people, have been sheltered."[9] Their year of service solidified rather than distanced their relationship to the Church. Once their military service was finished, possessed with a new sense of what was possible, both personally and for the Church they loved, the former soldiers continued to faithfully serve in any and all civic and Church capacities. Their military commitment only strengthened their resolve to fulfill their religious commitment, one they maintained throughout their lives. As John Hess described it, "I feel that the year's service . . . is one of the noblest and grandest acts of my life, for the reason that Israel was on the altar of sacrifice and the 'Mormon Battalion,' of which I was a member, went as the 'Ram in the Thicket,' and Israel was saved."[10]

Soon annual reunions were held by many of the former soldiers who, like Hess, reflected on their contribution to their country and the Church. On January 10, 1855, a reunion announcement was published in the *Deseret News* noting that "we will have a Ball and Supper on Feb. 6, 1855, in the Social Hall."[11] In addition to a general committee, county committees were also organized that included such former Battalion members as Ebenezer Brown, Thomas Dunn, Levi Hancock, John Hess, William Hyde, and William B. Pace. The announcement noted that the county committees "will immediately set about ascertaining the number of the members . . . [and] will take especial care to see that all wives of absent members and widows be invited. . . ."[12] About two weeks before the event, the *Deseret News* published a mini-editorial about the advertisement for the "Ball and Supper," in which it described the Mormon Battalion as "a proven band of

Battalion veterans, pictured here in 1896, met on numerous occasions to commemorate their service to their country and their church. (Courtesy of Church History Library.)

patriots."[13] In its recap of the service rendered by the Battalion soldiers, their sacrifice was extolled:

> At their country's call, approved by the counsel of President Brigham Young, this noble band of men, on a moment's warning, threw down their ox whips, entrusted their wives, children, and relatives to Israel's god, and to their brethren who were steeped in poverty through the oppression of mob violence, cheerfully wended their way to Fort Leavenworth, on the Missouri, from which they took up the long and weary march, through a hostile, barren and dreary region, for the Pacific coast. In addition to the testimony of Lt. Col. Cook of the U. S. A., we personally know the "Mormon Battalion" underwent and overcame more hardships in the same time, and with less complaint and disturbance than any body of troops, since the Revolution.[14]

In less than a decade, the remarkable sacrifice made by the Mormon Battalion had become legendary to Church members of that time. More than a century and a half later, Church members, collectively and individually, still honor that sacrifice.

Endnotes

1 Fleek, *History May be Searched in Vain*, 381.

2 Bigler, Journal, 7 October 1849, typescript, Church History Library.

3 Bigler, Diaries, HM57022, Journal Book B, 23 September 1850, Huntington Library, San Marino, California.

4 Brown, *Life of a Pioneer*, 110.

5 "Funeral of James S. Brown," *Deseret News*, March 31, 1903.

6 Boyle, Reminiscences and Diaries, 1846–1888, 254 , Church History Library.

7 Ibid., 255–256.

8 Charles William Stuart, "Henry G. Boyle biographical sketch, 18 January 1948," Church History Library.

9 Journal History, 5 April 1848, Church History Library.

10 Hess, Autobiography and journal, circa 1887–1895, 9, Church History Library.

11 "Mormon Battalion," *Deseret News*, January 18, 1855.

12 Ibid.

13 "Mormon Battalion," *Deseret News*, January 25, 1855.

14 Ibid.

INDEX

ABOUT THE AUTHORS

Michael N. Landon received a BA in history and political science from UCLA and an MA in public history from California State University, Sacramento. He is currently employed as an archivist in the Church History Department of The Church of Jesus Christ of Latter-day Saints and is a member of several historical and archival associations. He edited *The Journals of George Q. Cannon, Volume 1: To California in '49* and with Bill Slaughter authored *Trail of Hope: The Story of the Mormon Trail*. He and his wife, Loretta, reside in an historic home in Hooper, Utah. They have two children and seven grandchildren.

Brandon J. Metcalf is an archivist with the Church History Department of The Church of Jesus Christ of Latter-day Saints. He received a BA in history from Brigham Young University and an MA in public history from California State University, Sacramento. He and his wife, Angela, reside in Riverton, Utah, with their four children.

MORMON BATTALION

In compiling this list of Mormon Battalion soldiers, several sources have been consulted, including Mormon Battalion return lists for July 1846, Companies A and B; Mormon Battalion reports, February and March 1847; Morning report, September and October 1846, Company D; *Roster and Record of Iowa Soldiers in Miscellaneous Organizations of the Mexican War . . .*; "The Mormon Battalion, Iowa Volunteers: 1846–1848," *Piñon Whispers* (Southeastern Colorado Genealogical Society, 1998); Norma Ricketts, *The Mormon Battalion: U.S. Army of the West, 1846–1848* (Logan: Utah State University Press, 1996); Carl V. Larson, *A Database of the Mormon Battalion* (Salt Lake City: Mormon Battalion, 1997); and Historian's Office files created under the direction of Assistant Church Historian Andrew Jenson.

Despite referencing detailed and thorough research in primary and secondary works in an effort to identify every soldier who served in the Mormon Battalion, the existing contemporaneous and reconstructed rosters contain numerous inconsistencies that prevent a conclusive rendering of the roster. Discrepancies persist in the spelling of some surnames and in the criterion used in determining which of the men participated in at least part of the march. Although a sizable number of individuals accompanied the Mormon Battalion who were non-military, including many wives and children, this appendix focuses solely on the enlisted men.

U.S. Regular Military in the Mormon Battalion

Lt. Colonel James Allen (Commander from July–August 1846)
1st Lt. Andrew Jackson Smith (Commander from August–October 1846)
Lt. Colonel Philip St. George Cooke (Commander from October 1846–May 1847)
Lt. George Stoneman (Asst. Quartermaster Officer)
Dr. George B. Sanderson (Asst. Surgeon)
Dr. William McIntire (Asst. Surgeon)

Name / Company

Abbott, Joshua Chandler (D)
Adair, G. Wesley (C)
Adams, Orson Bennett (C)
Alexander, Horace Martin (B)
Allen, Albern (A)
Allen, Elijah (B)
Allen, Ezra Hela (C)
Allen, Franklin (B)
Allen, George A. (B)
Allen, John (E)
Allen, Rufus Chester (A)
Allred, James Riley (A)
Allred, James Tillmon
    Sanford (A)
Allred, Reddick (or Redick)
    Newton (A)
Allred, Reuben Warren (A)
Averett, Elisha (A)
Averett, Jeduthan (D)
Babcock, Lorenzo (C)

Badham, Samuel (D)
Bailey, Addison (C)
Bailey, James (A)
Bailey Jefferson (C)
Barger, William H. (D)
Barney, Walter, Sr. (C)
Barrus, Ruel (B)
Bates, Joseph William (E)
Beckstead, Gordon S. (A)
Beckstead, Orin Mortimer (A)
Beckstead, William Ezra (C)
Beddome, William (E)
Beers, William (E)
Bevan, James (A)
Bickmore, Gilbert (A)
Bigler, Henry William (B)
Bingham, Erastus, Jr. (B)
Bingham, Thomas, Sr. (B)
Binley, John Wesley (E)
Bird, William (B)

Blackburn, Abner (C)
Blanchard, Mervin S. (A)
Bliss, Robert S. (B)
Boley, Samuel (B)
Borrowman, John (B)
Boyd, George W. (D)
Boyd, William W. (D)
Boyle, Henry Green (C)
Brackenbury, Benjamin B. (B)
Brass, Benjamin (A)
Brazier, Richard (E)
Brimhall, John (C)
Brizzee, Henry Willard (D)
Bronson (or Brunson),
    Clinton Doneral (A)
Browett, Daniel (E)
Brown, Alexander (C)
Brown, Daniel (E)
Brown, Ebenezer (A)
Brown, Edmond Lee (E)

Brown, Francis (B)
Brown, James (Captain of
    Company C) (Captain
    of second detachment
    to Pueblo)
Brown, James P. (D)
Brown, James S. (D)
Brown, Jesse Sowell (C)
Brown, John (A)
Brown, William Walton (A)
Brownell, Russell Gideon (C)
Bryant, John Strange (A)
Buchanan, John (D)
Bulkley, Newman (E)
Bunker, Edward (E)
Burns, Thomas R. (E)
Burt, William (C)
Bush, Richard (B)
Bush, William H. (C)
Butterfield, Jacob Kemp (A)

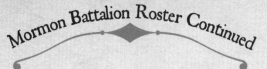
Button, Montgomery (D)

Bybee, John McCann (B)

Caldwell, Matthew (E)

Calkins, Alva C. (A)

Calkins, Edwin R. (A)

Calkins, James Wood (A)

Calkins, Sylvanus (A)

Callahan, Thomas William (B)

Calvert, John Hamaker (C)

Camp, James G. (B)

Campbell, Jonathan, Jr. (E)

Campbell, Samuel (E)

Canfield, Cyrus Culver (D)

Carpenter, Isaac (C)

Carpenter, William Henry (C)

Carter, Isaac Philo (B)

Carter, Richard (B)

Casper, William Wallace (A)

Casto, James B. (D)

Casto, William W. (D)

Catlin, George Washington (C)

Cazier, James (E)

Cazier, John (E)

Chapin, Samuel G. (E)

Chase, Abner (D)

Chase, Hiram Bentley (A)

Chase, John Darwin (B)

Cheney, Zacheus (B)

Church, Haden Wells (B)

Clark, Albert (E)

Clark, George Sheffer (B)

Clark, Joseph (E)

Clark, Joseph L. (A)

Clark, Lorenzo (A)

Clark, Riley Garner (A)

Clark, Samuel Gilman (E)

Clawson, John Reese (D)

Clift, James (C)

Clift, Robert (C)

Cole, James Barnet (D)

Coleman, George (A)

Collins, Robert H. (D)

Colton, Philander (B)

Compton, Allen (D)

Condit, Jeptha S. (C)

Coons, William A. (D)

Coray, William (B)

Covil, John Q. (C)

Cox, Amos (D)

Cox, Henderson (A)

Cox, John (E)

Cummings, George W. (E)

Curtis, Dorr Purdy (B)

Curtis, Foster (D)

Curtis, Josiah (A)

Dalton, Edward (C)

Dalton, Harry (C)

Dalton, Henry Simon (B)

Davis, Daniel Coon (Captain of Company E)

Davis, Eleaser (or Eleazer) (D)

Davis, James (D)

Davis, Sterling (D)

Davis, Walter L. (E)

Day, Abraham Eli (E)

Dayton, Willard T. (B)

Decker, Zachariah (or Zechariah) B. (A)

Dennett, Daniel Quimby (E)

Dobson, Joseph (A)

Dodge, Augustus Erastus (C)

Dodson, Eli (A)

Donald, Neal (C)

Douglas, James (D)

Douglas, Ralph (D)

Dunham, Albert (B)

Dunn, James (C)

Dunn, Thomas John (B)

Durphey (or Durphee), Francillo (C)

Dutcher, Thomas P. (B)

Dyke, Simon (or Simeon) (E)

Dykes, George Parker (D)

Earl, Jacob Sylpher (E)

Earl, James Calvin (A)

Earl, Justice C. (E)

Eastman, Marcus N. (B)

Egbert, Robert Cowden (A)

Elmer, Elijah (C)

Evans, Israel (B)

Evans, William (B)

Ewell, John Martin (E)

Ewell, William Fletcher (E)

Fairbanks, Henry (A)

Fatoute, Ezra (D)

Fellows, Hiram W. (C)

Ferguson, James (A)

Fife, John (C)

Fifield, Levi Joseph (C)

Finlay, Thomas B. (D)

Fletcher, Philander (D)

Follett, William A. (B)

Follett, William Tillmon (E)

Forbush, Loren E. (C)

Forney, Fredrick (E)

Forsgreen, John Erick (D)

Frazier, Thomas Leonard (D)

Fredrick (or Frederick), David Ira (A)

Freeman, Elijah Norman (B)

Frost, Lafayette N. (A)

Garner, David (A)

Garner, Philip (B)

Garner, William A. (B)

Gibson, Thomas (C)

Gifford, William W. (D)

Gilbert, John R. (D)

Gilbert, Thomas (D)

Glazier, Luther W. (E)

Glines, James Harvey (A)

Goodwin, Andrew (A)

Gordon, Gilman (A)

Gould, John Calvin (C)

Gould, Samuel J. (C)

Green, Ephraim (B)

Green, John W. (C)

Gribble, William (D)

Gully, Samuel (E)

Hampton, James (A)

Hancock, Charles Brent (C)

Hancock, George Washington (C)

Hancock, Levi Ward (E)

Hanks, Ebenezer (E)

Hanks, Ephraim Knowlton (B)

Harmon, Ebenezer (C)

Harmon, Lorenzo Frazer (C)

Harmon, Oliver Norton (E)

Harris, Robert, Jr. (E)

Harris, Silas (B)

Harrison, Isaac (E)

Hart, James Swarthout (E)

Haskell, George Nile (B)

Hatch, Meltiar (C)

Hatch, Orin (C)

Hawk, Nathan (B)

Hawk, William (B)

Hawkins, Benjamin T. (A)

Haws, Alpheus Peter (D)

Hendricks, William Dorius (D)

Hendrickson (or Henrichson), James (C)

Henrie, Daniel (D)

Hess, John Wells (E)

Hewett (or Hewitt), Eli B. (A)

Hickenlooper, William F. (A)

Hickmott, John (E)

Higgins, Alfred (D)

Higgins, Nelson (Captain of Company D) (Captain of first detachment to Pueblo)

Hinckley, Arza Erastus (B)

Hirons, James P. (D)

Hoagland, Lucas (D)

Hofheinz (or Hoffeins), Jacob (B)

Holdaway, Shedrick (or Shadrack) (C)

Holden, Elijah E. (A)

Holmes, Jonathan Herriman (D)

Holt, William (C)

Hopkins, Charles A. (E)

Hoskins, Henry (E)

Howell, Thomas C. (E)

Hoyt, Henry P. (A)

Hoyt, Timothy Sabin (A)

Hudson, Wilford Heath (A)

Hulet, Schuyler (or Skyler) (A)

Hulet, Sylvester (D)

Hunsaker, Abraham (D)

Hunt, Gilbert (A)

Hunt, Jefferson (Captain of Company A)

Hunt, Martial (or Marshall) (A)

Hunter, Edward (B)

Hunter, Jesse Divine (Captain of Company B)

Hunter, William (B)

Huntington, Dimick Baker (D)

Huntsman, Isaiah (B)

Hyde, William (B)

Ivie, Richard Anderson (A)

Ivie, Thomas C. (C)

Jackson, Charles A. (A)

Jackson, Henry Wells (D)

Jacobs, Bailey (E)

Jacobs, Sanford (D)

Jameson, Charles (E)

Johnson, Henry M. (A)

Johnson, Jarvis (C)

Johnstun, Jesse Walker (C)

Johnstun, William James (C)

Jones, David H. (B)

Jones, Nathaniel Vary (D)

Judd, Hyrum (or Hyram) (E)

Judd, Zadock (or Zadoc) Knapp (E)

Karren, Thomas (E)

Kelley, George (E)

Kelley, Milton (E)

Kelley, Nicholas (A)

Kelley, William (A)

Kenney, Loren E. (D)

Keysor, Guy Messiah (B)

Kibby, James (A)

King, John Morris (B)

Kirk, Thomas (B)

Knapp, Albert (E)

Lake, Barnabas (A)

Lamb, Lisbon (D)

Lance, William (E)

Landers, Ebenezer (C)

Lane, Lewis (D)

Larson, Thurston (C)

Laughlin, David Sanders (D)

Lawson, John (B)

Layton, Christopher (C)

Lemmon, James W. (A)

Lewis, Samuel (C)

Luddington, Elam (B)

Lytle, Andrew (E)